LET'S GO TO IRELAND

WHERE TO GO AND WHAT TO SEE

KELLI D. MARTIN

CONTENTS

INTRODUCTION

Feel the brisk wind tug at your coat as you stand on the precipice of the Cliffs of Moher, the Atlantic Ocean sprawling endlessly before you, its waves crashing against the rugged coastline, sending salty sprays into the air. This isn't just a visit; it's a journey into the heart of Ireland, where every corner tells a story, and every landscape feels like a brushstroke on a canvas of cultural richness and natural beauty.

This book, "Let's Go to Ireland: Where To Go and What To See," is designed to be your ultimate guide to exploring Ireland. It's crafted not just to inform but to immerse you in experiences that make Ireland uniquely enchanting—from the lively streets of Dublin, where history meets modernity, to the tranquil beauty of Connemara, where the land speaks to the soul.

What sets this guide apart is its focus on curated experiences, combining well-loved landmarks with hidden gems that only locals usually whisper about. The recommendations herein are more than just entries; they are stories carefully selected through personal adventures and thorough research, ensuring you experience the authenticity of Ireland.

The tone of this book is like that of a knowledgeable friend who has traversed these paths and is eager to share their secrets over a warm cup of coffee. With tips and insights, I aim to equip you with the confidence to explore this magnificent country, addressing common travel concerns and guiding you through creating a journey that aligns with your interests and exceeds your expectations.

Whether you're a history buff eager to tread the storied paths of ancient ruins, a nature lover looking to lose yourself in lush greenery, an adventurer ready to explore rugged trails, or a food enthusiast keen to savor local flavors, Ireland offers a plethora of experiences tailored just for you.

I understand that planning a trip to a new country can sometimes feel daunting. Rest assured, this book will simplify your planning process, ensuring that your Irish adventure is as seamless as it is memorable. You'll find practical advice on everything from navigating local transportation to finding the perfect accommodation —all tailored to fit a range of tastes and budgets.

So, consider this an invitation and a personal call to journey with me to the heart of Ireland. By the end of this book, you'll not only be prepared to explore the Emerald Isle but will do so with the excitement and ease of a seasoned traveler. Let's discover the magic of Ireland together. Let's make your Irish adventure unforgettable.

CHAPTER 1
THE PATH LESS TRAVELLED: UNCOVERING HIDDEN GEMS

As you turn the pages of this guide to uncover Ireland's most treasured corners, it's easy to visualize yourself meandering through landscapes so lush and vistas so vast they seem sprung from myth. Yet, Ireland's true allure lies in its panoramic views and the secrets nestled just beyond the well-trodden paths. In this chapter, we journey to places where the essence of Ireland sings through timeless villages, rugged terrains, and the enduring spirit of its people. These are the locales that invite you to slow down, breathe in the crisp air, and discover the Ireland that guidebooks often overlook but locals hold dear. Here, every stone, every path, and every wave tells a story, and I invite you to listen.

The Magic of Connemara: Beyond the National Park

Rugged Beauty Revealed

Connemara, a land of bog and heath, mountain and sea, is cele-brated not only for its National Park but for the wild beauty that stretches far beyond. Venture past the park's boundaries to discover a landscape that challenges the adventurous at heart and soothes the soul, seeking tranquility. Here, the mountains of Twelve Bens form a majestic backdrop to the intricate patchwork of small lakes and rivers that weave through the valleys. The quiet solitude of this region offers more than just a visual feast; it is a haven where you can walk for hours along trails where the only companions are the overhead calls of the peregrine falcons and red grouse. As you traverse this less frequented path, the untouched beauty of Connemara unfolds like a well-kept secret, each step offering a new vista, each turn revealing a landscape untouched by time.

Hidden Villages Explored

Within these rugged landscapes lie villages where time seems to have paused, allowing tradition to thrive. Places like Roundstone, a quaint fishing village, offer a glimpse into a life dictated by the tides and the catch. Here, you can meander through streets lined with artisan workshops, each a repository of local crafts, from hand-knotted fishing nets to the globally renowned Bodhrán drums. The warmth of the villagers is palpable, their stories a tapestry of folklore and fishing lore, willingly shared over a pint at O'Dowds, the local pub where the fire is always lit and the welcome always warm. These hidden villages, each with its unique charm, invite you to experience the slow rhythm of Irish rural life, untouched by the hustle of modernity.

Cultural Treasures Unearthed

Connemara is a feast for the eyes and a resonance for the ears, particularly through its language and music. This region is one of the last strongholds of the Irish language, and hearing it spoken here is like stepping back into another era, where each word carries the weight of history and culture. Traditional Irish music finds fertile ground in the pubs and on the streets. Impromptu sessions are a common delight, where locals and visitors alike gather to share in the joy of music. Instruments like the fiddle and tin whistle sing melodies that have been passed down through generations, each note a reflection of Connemara's soul.

Adventures Off the Beaten Path

For those who seek to immerse fully in Connemara's natural canvas, the region offers a plethora of activities that go beyond the usual tourist itineraries. Imagine yourself pony trekking across the rugged landscape, where the native Connemara ponies, with their sure-footedness and gentle demeanor, become your trusted guides through the heath. Or perhaps sea kayaking along the coast, where the clear waters open up to an underwater world of marine biodiversity, and the shores are frequented by seals sunning themselves on the rocks. These experiences connect you with nature and embed a sense of adventure into your visit, turning a simple trip into a memorable expedition across Connemara's untamed beauty.

As you explore these less trodden paths, each step reveals more than just the scenic beauty of Connemara—it unveils a deeper connection with a land rich in history, culture, and natural wonder. Here, away from the crowds, you find the true heart of Ireland, beating strongly amidst the mountains and the waves.

Sligo's Secret Beaches: A Surfer's Paradise Untold

Surfing Havens Identified

Sligo, with its rugged coastline and rolling waves, invites surfers who seek solitude from the crowded surfing spots found elsewhere. This lesser-known surfing haven boasts beaches like Strandhill and Enniscrone, where the waves offer both challenge and charm, perfect for those who wish to ride in peace. The allure of these beaches isn't just in their surfing quality but in their relative obscurity, providing a serene environment where one can connect with the sea without the interference of bustling crowds. Strandhill, just a few kilometers west of Sligo Town, greets its visitors with an expansive beach framed by dunes, offering waves that can challenge even seasoned surfers, especially during the robust swells of autumn. Meanwhile, Enniscrone, to the west, provides a more family-friendly surfing experience with its long, sandy beach that gently slopes into the Atlantic, making it an ideal spot for beginners and intermediate surfers alike. These beaches, with their consistent waves and uncrowded lineups, are jewels in Ireland's surfing crown, providing a pure and exhilarating surfing experience that is both rare and rewarding.

Local Surf Culture

The surf culture in Sligo is steeped in a camaraderie that transcends the usual competitive spirit found in more commercialized surf destinations. Here, local surf schools like the Northwest Surf School on Enniscrone Beach not only offer lessons but also foster a sense of community among surfers. The schools are often staffed by local surfers, whose lives are deeply intertwined with the tides and who carry stories of the sea that they share eagerly with anyone willing to listen. These instructors, many of whom have surfed the Atlantic waters since their youth, embody a passion for the sport that is contagious, often inspiring novices to become lifelong surf enthusiasts. Further enriching the local surf scene are legends like Barry Mottershead, a South African who has made Sligo his home and become one of the leading figures in big wave surfing in Ireland. Stories of his daring exploits riding the monstrous winter waves of the Sligo coast have become part of the local lore, contributing to the mystique and allure of surfing in this part of Ireland.

Natural Landscapes

The beaches of Sligo are not just surfing spots but stunning natural landscapes where the raw beauty of Ireland is on full display. The dramatic silhouette of Benbulben Mountain serves as an imposing backdrop to many of these beaches, its distinctive table-top shape formed millions of years ago during the Ice Age, providing a stark contrast to the rolling Atlantic waves. This interplay of mountain and sea is uniquely mesmerizing, offering moments of awe as one stands on the soft sand, board in hand, gazing at the ancient rock face while the ocean sings its eternal song. The beaches themselves, with their fine, clean sand and scattered rock pools, invite exploration and promise discovery, whether one is a surfer waiting for the next wave or a wanderer seeking the tranquility that only a beach can offer. The setting sun painting the skies in hues of orange and pink as it dips below the horizon, with Benbulben standing guard, is a sight that anchors itself in the memory, emblematic of Sligo's untamed beauty.

Eco-Conscious Exploration

In Sligo, the relationship between surfers and their environment is symbiotic, with a collective commitment to preserving the pristine condition of the beaches. Local surf schools and conservation groups often collaborate on initiatives aimed at maintaining beach cleanliness and ecological health. Regular beach clean-ups are organized, drawing volunteers who spend hours picking up litter washed ashore or left behind, ensuring that the beaches remain unspoiled for future generations. Additionally, there is a strong emphasis on educating surfers and visitors about the importance of minimizing their environmental impact, promoting practices such as using eco-friendly surf wax, avoiding single-use plastics, and respecting local wildlife habitats. This eco-conscious approach is deeply ingrained in the local surf culture, reflecting a broader recognition that the beauty of Sligo's beaches is a treasure to be safeguarded, a shared responsibility for all who are drawn to this surfer's paradise. The commitment to sustainability enhances the experience, ensuring that the exhilaration of riding Sligo's waves is matched by the gratification of contributing to the preservation of its natural landscapes.

The Burren's Untold Folklore: A Journey Through Time

Ancient History Uncovered

The Burren, a stark region in County Clare, is not merely a stretch of limestone karst landscape; it is a cradle of ancient history waiting to be explored. This area, characterized by its rock formations and contrasting lush flora, holds within its bounds a treasure trove of archaeological sites that date back over 6,000 years. Here, megalithic tombs such as the iconic Poulnabrone dolmen stand as silent sentinels of the past, their presence offering a direct connection to Ireland's Neolithic inhabitants. These tombs, carefully constructed with large slabs of limestone, serve as burial sites and markers of a sophisticated society that once mastered the art of survival in this seemingly inhospitable land. Nearby, stone forts like Caherconnell offer a glimpse into a later period of Irish history, where such structures were both dwellings and defensive outposts for families and their livestock. The strategic placement and intricate construction of these forts speak to a time when community and security were intricately linked, and the landscape played a central role in the daily lives of its inhabitants. Walking through these historic sites, one feels a profound sense of timelessness, as if the whispers of the past are etched into the stones themselves.

Folklore and Legends

The Burren is not only a ground of historical artifacts; it is also a rich repository of Irish folklore and legends, where every rock and hollow might tell a story. The landscape itself, with its eerie, moon-like appearance, has given rise to tales of otherworldly creatures and ancient heroes. One of the most enduring legends is that of O'Brien's Castle on Inchiquin Hill, where it is said faeries still gather using invisible doors nestled between the rocks. Local tales also recount the deeds of Fionn mac Cumhaill and the Fianna, ancient warriors said to roam the Burren, their feats of very intertwined with the very rocks that form the region's backbone. These stories passed down through generations, are mere myths; they are the threads that connect the past to the present, offering insights into the values and imaginations of the people who once walked this land. Engaging with these tales offers a deeper understanding of how history and folklore are woven together to create a tapestry rich with cultural significance.

Flora and Fauna

Amidst this stony silence, the Burren unexpectedly bursts into life with an astonishing variety of flora and fauna that defy the barren appearance of the limestone landscape. This region is renowned for its unique biodiversity, particularly the rare orchids and the Arctic-alpine plants that somehow thrive in the thin soil that gathers in the clints and grikes of the limestone pavement. The juxtaposition of Mediterranean, Arctic, and Alpine plants not only creates a botanist's paradise but also signifies the Burren's unusual microclimate, which allows such diversity to flourish. Conservation efforts are crucial in this area, as the delicate balance of this ecosystem can be easily disrupted. Numerous organizations and local groups coordinate to protect these species, ensuring that the area's natural heritage is preserved. This commitment to conservation safeguards the botanical richness and educates visitors on the importance of biodiversity and ecological responsibility.

Guided Walks and Trails

For those eager to delve into the Burren's rich tapestry of history, culture, and natural beauty, numerous guided tours and marked trails offer insightful explorations tailored to various interests and fitness levels. These guided walks, led by knowledgeable locals, do more than navigate the physical terrain; they offer narratives that illuminate the folklore, history, and ecological significance of the area. For an immersive experience, the Black Head Loop offers panoramic views of Galway Bay and the Aran Islands, encapsulating the harsh beauty and botanical wonders of the Burren. Alternatively, more focused thematic tours, such as those exploring ancient sacred sites or the region's biodiversity, allow for a deeper understanding of specific aspects of the Burren's heritage. These walking routes promote physical engagement with the landscape and foster an appreciation of how human history and natural history are profoundly interconnected in this unique region, making each step through the Burren a step through time itself.

Cobh: The Titanic's Last Port of Call

Titanic's Legacy

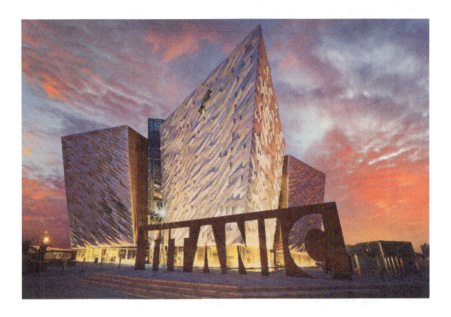

Cobh, formerly known as Queenstown, holds a poignant place in maritime history, notably as the last port of call for the RMS Titanic before its fateful journey across the Atlantic. This historic town, nestled in the harbor of Cork, offers more than picturesque views; it is a gateway to the past, to a moment frozen in time just before one of the most tragic maritime disasters unfolded. The Titanic Experience, housed in the original White Star Line Ticket Office, offers visitors an immersive journey into the lives of the passengers who boarded the Titanic from Cobh. Each visitor receives a boarding card bearing the name of an actual passenger, and as you walk through the reconstructed cabins and hear the stories, the experience culminates in the revelation of each passenger's fate. This powerful storytelling method connects you viscerally to the human aspects of the tragedy, making it more than a historical account but a deeply personal experience. Beyond the museum, various historical markers and memorials throughout the town, including the poignant Titanic Memorial Garden, provide spaces for reflection on the events of 1912, inviting you to ponder the dreams and despair of those who sailed into history from this very harbor.

Emigration Stories

Cobh's narrative is deeply intertwined with the history of Irish emigration. Over 2.5 million Irish departed from Cobh, driven by famine, conflict, and the pursuit of a better life, making it the single most significant point of emigration in the country. The Cobh Heritage Centre, located at the restored Victorian railway station, offers a gateway into this profound aspect of Irish history. The exhibition narrates the conditions that led to emigration, the journey itself, and the impact on the communities left behind as well as those that were formed in distant lands. Through personal letters, diaries, and belongings, the stories of emigration become vividly alive, mapping the emotional landscape of those who ventured into the unknown. This poignant tribute to the diaspora is not only a chronicle of the past but also a mirror reflecting the ongoing themes of migration and displacement in today's global context, making it incredibly relevant and moving.

Architectural Wonders

The architecture of Cobh is a visual feast, reflecting the town's rich history and vibrant community spirit. Dominating the skyline is St. Colman's Cathedral, a neo-Gothic marvel that took 47 years to complete. Its spire, towering over the town, serves as a beacon for those at sea and offers panoramic views of the harbor for those who venture up its tower. The cathedral's elaborate carvings, stunning stained glass, and a 49-bell carillon that rings out melodious tunes, enrich the cultural tapestry of Cobh. Down the hill from this majestic edifice, the streets of Cobh delight with rows of brightly painted houses, each color telling a story of the town's eclectic tastes and joyful community life. These vibrant facades, often adorned with historical plaques, lead down to the waterfront, creating a picturesque scene that invites leisurely exploration. Walking these streets, one experiences the architectural narrative of Cobh, from quaint worker's cottages to grandiose buildings, each adding a layer to the town's historical and aesthetic richness.

Maritime Adventures

Cobh's identity is inseparable from the sea, and the town offers a plethora of maritime activities that celebrate this bond. For those eager to experience the waters that have shaped this town's history, a harbor cruise provides not only breathtaking views but also a narrative of Cobh's maritime heritage, including tales of the many liners and naval ships that have anchored here. For a more hands-on experience, sailing tours are available, offering a chance to learn basic sailing techniques while exploring the various inlets and islands in the harbor. These tours often include stops at historical sites accessible only by water, such as the abandoned quarantine and convicts' stations on Spike Island, providing a unique perspective on Cobh's role in global maritime history. Additionally, sea angling trips can be arranged for those who wish to try their hand at fishing in these rich waters, with local skippers who share both their fishing expertise and their sea lore. Through these activities, Cobh's maritime legacy is not just observed but actively experienced, creating a dynamic connection between the visitor and the vast history of this storied harbor town.

Whispers from the Past: Exploring the Ruins of Hore Abbey

Serene Ruins Explored

Nestled in the shadow of the imposing Rock of Cashel, the ruins of Hore Abbey tell a tale of monastic life that has withstood the ravages of time. Originally founded by the Benedictine order in the 13th century before being handed over to the Cistercians, Hore Abbey's secluded location and dramatic backdrop make it a site of profound historical and architectural significance. Unlike its towering neighbor, the Rock of Cashel, Hore Abbey offers a more untouched, raw glimpse into the past, its sprawling ruins more reflective of the solitary monastic lifestyle. Each stone and collapsed wall within the Abbey grounds whispers stories of a bygone era, from the daily chants of monks to the silent, meditative existence that once defined life here. The architecture, with remnants of the cloister, refectory, and the living quarters, invites visitors to wander through and contemplate the lives of those who once called this place home. The absence of commercialization here makes Hore Abbey a place where history feels palpable, enveloped in the tranquility that comes from being slightly removed from the usual tourist paths.

Photographic Gem

For photography enthusiasts and casual visitors alike, Hore Abbey offers endlessly compelling subjects, particularly in the interplay of light and shadow that dances across the ruins at different times of the day and year. Capturing the perfect photograph here involves observing how the sun casts dramatic silhouettes of the arches and towers during the golden hours of sunrise and sunset. The changing seasons offer varied palettes; lush green fields in spring and summer contrast sharply with the stark, bare stone, while autumn and winter clothe the landscape in softer, muted tones that speak of quiet decay and the passage of time. Photographers will find that early morning mist creates an ethereal quality, with the Abbey ruins shrouded in a ghostly fog that enhances its mystique. Conversely, late afternoon brings a golden glow that bathes the stone in warm light, highlighting the texture and details of the ancient masonry, perfect for those seeking to capture a sense of enduring majesty despite inevitable ruin.

Local Lore

The stories and legends that swirl around Hore Abbey add a rich layer of mystique to its already captivating presence. One prevalent tale tells of the Abbey's transition from the Benedictine to the Cistercian order, allegedly spurred by a dream of the Benedictine abbot who foresaw his own monks attempting to murder him. This narrative of betrayal and prophecy is woven into the fabric of the Abbey, casting a somber shadow over its serene surroundings and inviting visitors to look deeper into the nooks and crannies that might have housed such dark secrets. Another local legend hints at hidden passages connecting Hore Abbey to the Rock of

Cashel, supposed pathways for monks seeking refuge or secret meetings. These stories, whether rooted in fact or fable, are recounted with gusto by local guides and are integral to the experience of the Abbey, rendering it not just a site of historical interest, but a place where the past feels dynamically intertwined with the present.

A Quiet Retreat

In a world that moves at a relentless pace, Hore Abbey offers a rare retreat into silence and solitude. Visitors here are struck by the peace that envelops the area, a stark contrast to the more frequented sites nearby. This tranquility makes Hore Abbey a perfect spot for those seeking not just to tour but to truly absorb and reflect. The open fields surrounding the ruins invite you to sit and gaze at the horizon, perhaps with a book or simply your thoughts for company. The sense of solitude is profound, not loneliness but a comforting aloneness that the Abbey's monks might have once cherished. It's this peaceful atmosphere that calls to those who seek a moment to disconnect from the world and reconnect with themselves amidst whispers of history and the timeless beauty of nature's embrace.

Culinary Delights of Cork's English Market

Local and Artisanal Foods

Nestled in the heart of Cork City, the English Market, a melting pot of culinary diversity, offers an authentic taste of Ireland's gastronomic richness. This historic market, renowned for its vibrant atmosphere and quality produce, stands as a testament to Cork's flourishing culinary scene. As you wander through the bustling aisles, you are met with an array of local and artisanal products that paint a delicious picture of the region's food heritage. Here, the air is rich with the aromas of freshly baked artisan bread, local cheeses, and the distinct scent of smoked fish. Each stall has its own story, often tied to family-run businesses that have passed down through generations, their products reflecting a commitment to quality and a passion for food. For example, the renowned O'Connell Fish, where the O'Connell family has been offering the freshest seafood for over a century, showcases the best of local waters with offerings like smoked salmon and plump oysters, each bite a testament to Ireland's seafood prowess. Similarly, the stalls of local butchers are a carnivore's delight, with traditionally cured meats and handmade sausages that celebrate Ireland's rich farming heritage. The market is not just a place to shop; it is a vibrant hub of local culture, where each vendor's produce tells a story of Ireland's lush fields, wild oceans, and the meticulous craft that transforms simple ingredients into culinary treasures.

Tasting Journey

Embarking on a self-guided tour of the English Market is akin to taking a culinary journey through Ireland's past and present. This exploration is an adventure of flavors, where each stall offers a unique taste of both traditional Irish foods and contemporary fare. Begin at the Farmgate Café, located within the market, where the menu is a tribute to the produce sold by the vendors below. Here, a dish of tripe and onions, a Cork specialty, offers a direct connection to local culinary history, while a plate of artisanal cheese and chutney sourced from the market vendors provides a snapshot of modern Irish tastes. As you continue through the market, indulge in a tasting spree: sample the renowned spiced beef, a Cork delicacy especially popular at Christmas, or savor the richness of freshly churned butter from a local dairy stall. Each taste satisfies the palate and deepens the understanding of Ireland's culinary evolution, from time-honored recipes to innovative dishes that fuse international flavors with local ingredients. This journey through the market is an informal yet deeply informative way to engage with the food culture of Cork, offering insights into the meticulous care with which these foods are prepared and the communal spirit that they foster among locals and visitors alike.

Market History

The English Market, with its ornate entrances and vaulted ceilings, holds within its architecture over two centuries of history. Established in 1788, the market has survived through periods of immense social and economic change, standing as a witness to Ireland's evolving history. The market was designed to elevate the shopping experience of Cork's citizens, with an emphasis on providing a clean, organized space for the transaction of quality goods—a stark contrast to the chaotic street markets of the time. Throughout the years, it has seen the rise and fall of empires, survived fires, and undergone numerous renovations, each adding layers to its historical tapestry. The resilience of the market is perhaps best illustrated by its survival and rejuvenation after a fire in 1980, which led to extensive restorations, ensuring that its historical charm was preserved while modernizing its facilities to meet contemporary needs. This blend of the old and the new makes the market not just a shopping venue but a historical landmark that offers a tangible connection to Cork's past. The market's ability to adapt and thrive mirrors the city's resilience and innovation, symbolizing community strength and continuity.

Meet the Vendors

The soul of the English Market undoubtedly resides in its vendors, each one a custodian of culinary skills and local knowledge. Engaging with these vendors enriches the shopping experience and provides insights into the craftsmanship involved in their trades. Take, for instance, Tom Durcan, known for his spiced beef, who can often be found at his stall sharing recipes and tips on how to cook this local specialty. Or visit Isabelle Sheridan at On The Pig's Back, a French-native who has made Cork her home, offering a fusion of Irish and French cheese and charcuterie, her stall a testament to the cultural melding that characterizes modern Irish cuisine. These interactions are invaluable; the vendors not only sell their products but also their passion and stories, making every purchase a personal exchange. They are eager to recommend the best ways to enjoy their products, often suggesting pairings or sharing traditional cooking methods, thus providing a deeper appreciation of the food's cultural significance. This personal touch transforms the market from a mere shopping venue into a vibrant community space, where food serves as a medium for cultural exchange and culinary discovery.

In this bustling marketplace, where the past meets the present in every corner, each stall offers more than just food—it offers a story, a taste of Ireland's bountiful produce and the rich tapestry of its culinary heritage. Here, in the heart of Cork, the English Market stands as a beacon of local pride and gastronomic delight, inviting all who visit to partake in its offerings and leave with a piece of Ireland's culinary soul.

CHAPTER 2
CULTURAL ENCOUNTERS: LIVING THE IRISH WAY

As you weave through the verdant landscapes and bustling cities of Ireland, a deeper journey awaits—one that invites you to immerse yourself in the vibrant tapestry of Irish culture. Beyond the scenic vistas and historic landmarks, Ireland's true spirit pulses in its rich traditions, particularly through its music. In this chapter, we delve into the heart of Irish cultural life, exploring the rhythms and melodies that have echoed across the ages. Here, you'll not just observe but actively participate in traditions that continue to shape the Irish identity, forging a connection that resonates long after your visit ends.

A Night to Remember: Experiencing Trad Music in Doolin

Musical Heritage

Nestled on the rugged west coast of Ireland, Doolin is a small village with a towering reputation as the epicenter of traditional Irish music. Known affectionately as the capital of Irish trad music, Doolin offers more than just picturesque views; it is a gateway to an immersive musical experience that connects you to Ireland's cultural heart. The music here is a lifeline, passed down through generations, each tune and each song steeped in the stories of the land. As you step into Doolin, the lilting melodies of fiddles and the rhythmic beats of bodhráns invite you to explore this rich musical heritage that is as vibrant today as it was centuries ago. This village, though small, plays a significant role in preserving and celebrating traditional Irish music, hosting musicians and music lovers from around the world who come to partake in this dynamic cultural exchange.

Pub Sessions

The essence of Doolin's musical culture is best experienced through its legendary pub sessions. As night falls, the pubs along Fisher Street, such as McGann's and O'Connor's, become the beating heart of the village, buzzing with energy and filled with the sounds of traditional Irish music. Here, musicians gather around small tables, instruments in hand, ready to weave a tapestry of melodies that tell tales of joy, sorrow, and life's simple pleasures. These sessions are spontaneous, with musicians often joining in impromptu, creating a unique and authentic atmosphere where the barrier between performer and audience dissolves. As a visitor, you are welcomed into this warm embrace, where the clinking of glasses accompanies the swell of music, and the air is thick with the camaraderie and communal spirit that is characteristic of Irish pub culture. The instruments—fiddles, tin whistles, accordions, and bodhráns—each play their part in creating a symphony that resonates with the soul of Ireland.

Festivals and Events

Doolin's musical landscape is punctuated throughout the year with festivals and events that celebrate its heritage and attract fans from all corners of the globe. One of the highlights is the Russell Memorial Weekend in February, a festival that honors the legendary Russell family, whose members were pivotal in shaping Doolin's musical identity. Another key event is the Doolin Folk Festival, which takes place in June and features a lineup of both established and emerging Irish artists. These festivals not only showcase the depth and breadth of Irish musical talent but also create a festive atmosphere where music flows from every corner, inviting everyone to dance, sing, and celebrate the enduring legacy of Irish trad music. Attending these events offers you a deeper understanding of the importance of music in community life in Doolin, providing a window into the collective soul of the village.

Musical Discovery

For those inspired to delve deeper into the world of Irish music, Doolin offers numerous opportunities to learn and engage directly with this art form. Many local pubs and music schools host workshops and informal sessions where beginners are taught the basics of traditional instruments by seasoned musicians. These workshops provide a hands-on experience that is both educational and deeply personal, allowing you to not only learn about the music but become an active participant in its ongoing tradition. Whether it's mastering the art of the tin whistle, trying your hand at the bodhrán, or simply learning to appreciate the subtleties of each tune, these experiences enrich your understanding of Irish culture and add a profound layer of meaning to your visit. As you hold the instruments, feel their weight, and coax out melodies guided by skilled musicians, you become part of a cultural continuum, playing notes that have resonated through the ages—a truly unforgettable encounter with Ireland's living history.

The Gaelic Games: Experiencing Hurling and Gaelic Football

Introduction to Gaelic Games

Stepping into the realm of Gaelic games opens up a vibrant chapter of Irish culture, where the ancient sports of hurling and Gaelic football are not just games but celebrations of heritage and community spirit. Hurling, one of the world's fastest field sports, is an exhilarating blend of speed, skill, and ancient tradition, involving a small ball called a sliotar and a curved wooden stick known as a hurley. Gaelic football, on the other hand, mixes elements of soccer, rugby, and basketball, creating a dynamic game that captivates with its pace and physicality. Both sports are governed by the Gaelic Athletic Association (GAA), an organization deeply embedded in the social fabric of Ireland, dedicated not only to promoting these sports but also to fostering a sense of identity and pride across generations. These games are more than mere athletic contests; they are a living legacy, a connective tissue that binds communities and echoes the resilience and strength of the Irish people. Attending a match or participating in these sports offers a unique window into the soul of Ireland, where passion, tradition, and community converge on the pitch.

Attend a Match

Imagine yourself amidst the electrifying atmosphere of a hurling or Gaelic football match, where the air is thick with anticipation and the stands are a sea of team colors. Attending one of these matches is a must-do experience, offering not only the thrill of the game but also a chance to engage with Irish culture at its most vibrant. Croke Park in Dublin, the spiritual home of Gaelic games, provides the perfect backdrop for this encounter. Before you go, familiarizing yourself with the basic rules will enhance your experience. In hurling, watch how players masterfully balance the sliotar on their hurleys while sprinting towards the goal. In Gaelic football, observe the blend of kicking, hand-passing, and strategic plays that drive the game forward. Engage with local fans, who are usually more than willing to explain finer points and share their fervor for the game. The communal experience of cheering, celebrating, or groaning in unison with thousands of fans offers an authentic taste of Irish passion and pride, making you feel part of something much larger than just a spectator at a sports event.

Community Involvement

The impact of Gaelic games stretches far beyond the stadiums, seeping into Ireland's towns and villages, where local clubs are the heartbeat of the community. Within these clubs, individuals of all ages unite not merely for the game itself but to revel in, bolster, and perpetuate age-old traditions. The role of these clubs is multifaceted—they are centers for athletic training, community gatherings, and cultural preservation. Youth teams are particularly vibrant, with children taking up hurling and Gaelic football from a young age, learning the skills of the games and the values of teamwork, respect, and perseverance. Volunteering at these clubs, whether helping with coaching, organizing events, or maintaining facilities, is a common practice among members, reflecting a community-oriented approach that is integral to the sustainability of the games. These grassroots engagements provide a foundation for personal and communal growth, weaving the love for Gaelic games into the daily fabric of life in Ireland.

Historical Context

The Gaelic Athletic Association (GAA), founded in 1884, has been pivotal in nurturing the Gaelic games to their current revered status. Established during a time of growing Irish nationalism, the GAA played a crucial role in the revival of native Irish sports, which had been suppressed under British rule. By promoting hurling and Gaelic football, the GAA provided a cultural rallying point for the Irish people, a means of expressing national identity and pride. The association's motto, "A nation that plays together, stays together," encapsulates its mission to strengthen community ties and foster a sense of Irish identity through sports. The historical significance of the GAA is evident in how it intertwined sports, culture, and politics, making Gaelic games a powerful symbol of Ireland's struggle for independence and its enduring spirit. Understanding this context adds a layer of depth to watching a hurling or Gaelic football match, transforming it from a mere sporting event into an act of cultural engagement that resonates with the echoes of history.

Through this journey into the world of Gaelic games, you're not merely spectators of hurling and Gaelic football's exhilarating dynamics but also participants in the vibrant tapestry of Irish culture and tradition. These games encapsulate the spirit of a nation that values tradition, community, and the sheer joy of play, offering a profound way to experience the true essence of Irish culture.

Literary Dublin: A Bloomsday Walk Through Joyce's City

Joyce's Dublin

Dublin, a city woven with the threads of literary genius, offers a unique experience to walk through the pages of history, tracing the steps of one of its most celebrated sons, James Joyce. To wander through Joyce's Dublin is to navigate a labyrinth of cobblestone streets and historic landmarks that leap from the pages of his masterpieces, particularly the epic "Ulysses." This literary pilgrimage begins at 15 Usher's Island, the setting of the poignant "The Dead," where the palpable echoes of the past mingle with the rhythms of daily life. From here, a short stroll along the quays of the River Liffey brings you to the heart of the city, where the iconic Ha'penny Bridge leads to the bustling thoroughfares Joyce once roamed. A visit to Sweny's Pharmacy, now a quaint shop preserved almost as it was in Joyce's time, allows you to immerse yourself in the sensory details of "Ulysses," with lemon soap still available, a fragrant memento of Leopold Bloom's visit within the novel.

Continuing on, the tour leads you past Trinity College, where Joyce studied, imbuing you with a sense of the intellectual fervor that shapes much of his work. The nearby National Library of Ireland offers another key stop, where Joyce's character Stephen

Dedalus expounds his aesthetic theories—an ideal place for contemplation and connection with Dublin's literary heritage. The walk culminates at Davy Byrne's pub on Duke Street—famous for its mention in "Ulysses" and an essential stop for refreshment and reflection on the journey through Joyce's city. Each location, steeped in literary and historical significance, offers a deeper understanding of Joyce's work and the city that so profoundly influenced his literary landscape.

Bloomsday Celebrations

Every year on June 16th, Dublin transforms into a living narrative to celebrate Bloomsday, marking the day depicted in "Ulysses." This citywide event sees Joyceans, from the curious to the devoted, donning early twentieth-century attire—straw boater hats and long skirts—to honor Joyce's detailed rendering of Edwardian Dublin. The festivities are a vibrant tapestry of readings, dramatizations, and musical performances, each bringing chapters of "Ulysses" to life against the backdrop of its real-world settings. One of the day's highlights includes public readings from "Ulysses" at key landmarks like Sandymount Strand, where key scenes from the novel unfold. Performers and participants engage in lively discussions, debates, and recitations, creating a communal literary experience that resonates with both casual attendees and Joyce scholars. The air is filled with the music of bygone eras, and impromptu performances turn ordinary street corners into stages for reenacting Joyce's narrative. Bloomsday transcends mere celebration of Joyce's literary legacy, weaving together visitors and Dubliners, and connecting diverse generations and cultures in a shared literary embrace.

Literary Landmarks

Beyond Joyce, Dublin's streets are a palimpsest of literary history, with landmarks commemorating writers such as Samuel Beckett, Oscar Wilde, and W.B. Yeats, each adding layers to the city's rich literary heritage. A visit to the Dublin Writers Museum in Parnell Square offers a comprehensive overview of the city's literary legends, housing rare first editions, personal letters, and historic artifacts. Nearby, the beautifully restored Oscar Wilde House on Merrion Square opens a window into the early life of one of Ireland's wittiest playwrights. For those drawn to the mystic and the gothic, St. Patrick's Cathedral offers a connection to Jonathan Swift, author of "Gulliver's Travels," who once served as its dean. Each of these sites contributes to a deeper appreciation of Dublin as a city that has continuously inspired and been shaped by literary greats, reinforcing its status as a UNESCO City of Literature.

Modern Literary Scene

Dublin's literary legacy is not confined to the past; the city's contemporary literary scene is vibrant and thriving, with new voices rising to narrate the complexities of modern Ireland. Bookshops like The Winding Stair and Chapters host readings and signings by local authors, fostering a community centered around the written word. The annual International Literature Festival Dublin brings together writers, poets, and storytellers from around the world, offering a platform for dialogue and exchange that enriches the city's cultural landscape. Contemporary Irish authors like Sally Rooney, Colm Tóibín, and Eimear McBride, continue to push the boundaries of literature, exploring themes of identity, belonging, and transformation. Their works, celebrated both at home and internationally, are a testament to the enduring vibrancy of Dublin's literary scene, ensuring that the city's tradition of storytelling continues to evolve, captivating the imaginations of readers and writers alike for generations to come.

The Craft of Irish Whiskey: Distillery Visits and Tastings

Whiskey's Roots

Irish whiskey, with its smooth finish and complex flavors, carries with it a storied past that intertwines deeply with Ireland's history and culture. The tale of Irish whiskey began over a thousand years ago, influenced by the ancient distillation techniques brought to Ireland by traveling monks. It is believed that Ireland housed the first distillation of whiskey on the British Isles, making it a pioneer in the craft. The word 'whiskey' itself derives from the Irish term "uisce beatha," meaning "water of life," a testament to the spirit's significance in Irish heritage. Over the centuries, Irish whiskey flourished, becoming globally renowned by the 18th and 19th centuries. Distilleries like Old Bushmills, which claims to be the world's oldest licensed distillery established in 1608, played pivotal roles in developing the unique characteristics of Irish whiskey, including its triple distillation process which imparts a smoother texture compared to its counterparts. The 20th century brought challenges, with wars and prohibition impacting production. However, the resurgence of interest in craft spirits in recent decades has heralded a new golden age for Irish whiskey, with both historical distilleries and new artisans crafting whiskeys that honor traditional methods while embracing innovative techniques.

Distillery Tours

For enthusiasts eager to delve into the world of Irish whiskey, a visit to one of the many distilleries offers an enlightening glimpse into the crafting process and the chance to taste premium whiskeys. The Jameson Distillery on Bow Street in Dublin provides a captivating tour where you can engage with the history of one of Ireland's most iconic whiskey brands. The tour includes a walk through the old distillery, a comparative whiskey tasting, and even a chance to blend your own take-home whiskey. For those venturing outside Dublin, the Kilbeggan Distillery in County Westmeath offers an experience steeped in history where you can view the old waterwheel and the original stills that have been producing whiskey since 1757. Meanwhile, the Teeling Distillery, a newer establishment in Dublin's historic Liberties district, offers a modern take on whiskey production with their innovative cask aging techniques, showcasing how new players are evolving the Irish whiskey narrative. Each distillery visit provides a unique perspective, from the historical to the contemporary, inviting you to not only learn about the rich past of Irish

whiskey but also to experience firsthand the passion and craftsmanship that goes into each bottle.

Tasting Notes

Understanding the subtleties of whiskey tasting can significantly
enhance your appreciation of this storied spirit. When embarking
on a whiskey tasting, it's important to engage all your senses.
Begin by examining the whiskey's color, which can range from
light gold to deep amber, often hinting at the type of cask used
and the length of aging. Swirl the whiskey gently in the glass to
release its diverse aromas. Take a moment to inhale deeply; Irish
whiskey typically offers a range of smells from fresh fruity notes
to deep spicy undertones, depending on its composition and
aging process. When tasting, let the whiskey wash over your
tongue slowly, noticing the initial flavors, the mid-palate experience, and the finish. Good Irish whiskey should have a balance of
sweetness, often derived from malt, with varying degrees of

warmth from spices and smoothness from its triple distillation. Notes of vanilla, caramel, or wood might be detectable, results of its maturation in oak barrels. Each sip should reveal layers of flavor, crafted carefully by the distiller's skill and choices.

Pairing Food and Whiskey

Pairing whiskey with food can transform a simple meal into a gastronomic adventure, elevating both the dish and the spirit. Irish whiskey, with its versatile flavor profile, pairs splendidly with a variety of foods. For a classic combination, try pairing a smooth, mellow Irish whiskey with smoked salmon; the whiskey's vanilla tones and the salmon's rich flavors complement each other beautifully. For cheese lovers, a sharper whiskey with spicy notes can be paired with aged cheddar, where the fat in the cheese balances the whiskey's heat, enhancing its deeper flavors. If you're enjoying a hearty meal of Irish stew, a robust whiskey with woodsy or earthy undertones makes an excellent companion, echoing the rustic flavors of the stew. For dessert, a whiskey with hints of caramel and chocolate pairs delightfully with a warm apple pie, creating a comforting, indulgent experience. These pairings bring out the best in the whiskey and introduce a delightful layer to dining, making each bite and each sip a discovery of complementary flavors.

The Art of Irish Storytelling: An Evening by the Hearth

Storytelling Tradition

In the warm glow of a hearth, nestled in a cozy corner of Ireland, the age-old tradition of storytelling comes to life, weaving a tapestry that connects the past with the present. The Irish, known for their rich oral heritage, have passed down tales from generation to generation, using storytelling as a means to entertain, educate, and preserve their culture. This tradition stretches back to the ancient Celts, who revered their bards and storytellers, viewing them as custodians of history and folklore. These story-tellers, or seanchaís, held a place of honor in society, their tales of epic battles, mystical creatures, and legendary heroes resonating through the ages. Today, the essence of this tradition remains vibrant, with modern storytellers embracing these time-honored tales while interweaving contemporary narratives that speak to the conditions and challenges of current times. Storytelling sessions, often held in public houses or at community gatherings, provide a space where the young and old can connect, the rhythm and lilt of the spoken word strengthening communal ties and fostering a shared sense of identity. As you sit and listen, the barriers of time erode, linking you to the listeners who once gath-ered around firesides under starlit skies, enraptured by the power of spoken words.

Storytelling Venues

Across Ireland, numerous venues and events celebrate this storied practice, allowing visitors to immerse themselves in the art of storytelling. One of the most enchanting places to experience this is The Stag's Head in Dublin, a historic pub where weekly story-telling sessions transport listeners to other realms. Here, under the dimly lit ambiance and rustic beams, storytellers regale the audience with tales that are as much a part of Ireland as its rolling green hills. In the west, The Crane Bar in Galway offers a more intimate setting, where the stories told are often interlaced with traditional music, the melodies heightening the narrative's emotional pull. For those visiting in autumn, the Cape Clear Island International Storytelling Festival presents a unique opportunity to experience storytelling in a dramatic island setting, with the Atlantic as a backdrop. This festival gathers some of the world's best storytellers, their tales echoing the ancient lore of the land and seas. Each venue, with its distinct charm and character, serves as a gateway to the past and a bridge to the universal human experience, narrated through the unique lens of Irish culture.

Famous Irish Tales

As you delve deeper into the world of Irish storytelling, you encounter a realm where legends such as Cú Chulainn and Fionn mac Cumhaill live and breathe. These tales, rooted in Ireland's mythological cycles, are not mere stories; they are woven into the fabric of Irish identity. Cú Chulainn, the great hero of the Ulster Cycle, known for his superhuman strength and tragic destiny, captures the imagination with his feats of bravery and heart-wrenching loyalty. His stories, along with those of Fionn mac Cumhaill, the wise and cunning leader of the Fianna, are recounted with reverence and awe, their complexities reflecting the values and struggles of the Celtic people. These narratives, rich with adventure and mysticism, offer more than entertainment; they serve as moral and philosophical guides, exploring themes of honor, heroism, and the eternal battle between good and evil. Understanding these stories provides a deeper appreciation of the Irish psyche, revealing a culture that values wit, wisdom, and the eternal search for meaning.

Participatory Experiences

For those inspired by Ireland's storytelling heritage, participating in a storytelling workshop or an open-mic night offers a chance to engage actively with this tradition. These events, often held in community centers or local pubs, invite you to not only listen but also to share your own stories. Whether recounting a personal memory or a fictional tale, the act of storytelling fosters a deep connection with others, bridging differences through the universal language of narrative. In cities like Cork and Limerick, storytelling workshops provide tools and techniques for effective storytelling, encouraging participants to find their own voice and style. These workshops emphasize the importance of pacing, tone, and emotion in storytelling, equipping you with the skills to captivate an audience. Meanwhile, open-mic nights celebrate the spontaneity and diversity of storytelling, where stories from various cultures and perspectives come together, enriching the tapestry of human experience. Here, in the shared act of story-telling, you find a sense of belonging and community, your narra-tive thread joining the larger story of Ireland itself.

Farm to Fork: A Day with an Irish Farmer

Agricultural Heritage

The lush green fields of Ireland are not just a feast for the eyes; they are the backbone of the nation's rich agricultural heritage, deeply rooted in both the economy and the culture of the land. Farming in Ireland is more than an occupation; it's a way of life that has sustained generations. Across rolling hills and fertile plains, farmers engage in practices that are increasingly tilting towards organic and sustainable methods, responding to global needs and local traditions with equal fervor. This transition to sustainable farming reflects a broader commitment to preserving the landscape that defines Ireland—its verdant pastures, its rugged coastlines, and its wild, untamed beauty. Organic farming, in particular, plays a crucial role in this narrative, reducing envi-ronmental impact and enhancing biodiversity. It involves crop rotation, natural pest controls, and a strict ban on synthetic chemicals, ensuring that the produce tastes better and supports the well-being of the environment and the consumers. By participating in this sustainable cycle, Irish farmers continue their ancestors' legacy, fostering a connection to the land that is both ancient and vitally contemporary.

Farm Visits

For those who wish to experience this deep, earthy connection, a visit to one of Ireland's many working farms offers a hands-on glimpse into the country's agricultural life. These visits can vary from a few hours to a full day and often culminate in a stay at a farm guesthouse. Imagine starting your day with the crow of the rooster, participating in the daily routines of a dairy farmer, or walking the fields of an organic produce farm, each activity offering insights not just into farming, but into a way of life. In County Kerry, Kissane Sheep Farm offers visitors the chance to witness sheepdog demonstrations, where the intelligence of the dogs and the skill of the farmer are on full display. Further north, in County Meath, Causey Farm opens its doors to those interested in a more interactive experience, where you can try your hand at bog jumping, bread baking, or even milking a cow. These experiences are designed to educate and to immerse you in the pastoral beauty and the agricultural rhythm of rural Ireland, creating memories that are as enriching as they are delightful.

From Milk to Cheese

A quintessential part of any agricultural tour in Ireland is the cheese-making process, a craft that has been perfected over centuries. At farms like the Ballymaloe Cookery School in County Cork, you can witness this artistry first-hand. The journey from milk to cheese begins with the morning milking, where the freshness of the milk is paramount. This milk is then pasteurized or sometimes left raw for certain types of cheeses, and mixed with rennet to start the curdling process. What follows is a meticulous practice of cutting, cooking, and washing the curd, each step carefully managed to influence the texture and flavor of the cheese. After the curds are drained and pressed into molds, they are aged in controlled environments to develop depth and character. Cheese-making workshops often end with a tasting session, where you can savor the rich, creamy textures of freshly made cheeses, each bite a testament to the skill and dedication of Irish farmers. This journey from milk to cheese not only highlights the craft involved in dairy farming but also showcases the passion for quality and tradition that characterizes Irish agriculture.

Seasonal Activities

The rhythm of farm life in Ireland is governed by the seasons, each bringing its own set of activities and celebrations. In spring, the countryside is dotted with newborn lambs, and farms often welcome visitors to witness lambing first-hand, an experience that connects you to the cycle of life that drives agricultural practice. Summer brings with it the promise of lush growth, making it the perfect time for farm tours that explore the cultivation of crops and the maintenance of the stunning floral landscapes that many Irish farms boast. Autumn is harvest time, a period of bustling activity where you can participate in harvesting apples for cider making or potatoes for storing through the winter. Many farms celebrate this time of year with harvest festivals, where the bounty of the land is shared and celebrated with music, dance, and plenty of farm-fresh food. As winter approaches, activities shift towards preparation for the colder months—preserving fruits, repairing farm equipment, and, of course, enjoying the quiet beauty of the Irish countryside under a blanket of frost. These seasonal activities provide a glimpse into the practical aspects of farming and also into the cultural rituals that accompany each phase of the agricultural calendar, offering a deeper understanding and appreciation of the land and its keepers.

Exploring the agricultural roots of Ireland gives you a profound appreciation for the land and the people who cultivate it. From the organic fields that thrive under the care of dedicated farmers to the ancient practice of cheese-making that continues to delight palates, each experience enriches your understanding of this green island. As you participate in daily farm activities, witness the sustainable practices firsthand, and celebrate the seasons of harvest, you connect with a part of Ireland that is both timeless and dynamically engaged in the modern world. This chapter offers not just a journey through Ireland's farming traditions but an invitation to engage deeply with the land, its products, and its people.

CHAPTER 3

NATURE'S WONDERS: IRELAND'S OUTDOOR ESCAPES

Imagine stepping into a living canvas, where every path leads to breathtaking vistas and every breath of fresh, crisp air enriches your soul. In Ireland, nature crafts an exquisite tapestry of colors, textures, and sounds, inviting you to step off the beaten path and explore its pristine beauty. From the rugged cliffs that guard the coast to the lush forests that blanket the hills, Ireland's landscapes are not just to be seen but experienced. This chapter invites you to lace up your boots, ready your senses, and journey through Ireland's great outdoors, where adventure and tranquility go hand in hand.

Hiking the Wicklow Way: Ireland's Garden

Trail Highlights

The Wicklow Way offers some of the most picturesque and engaging hiking experiences in Ireland, presenting a blend of rugged mountain trails and serene forest walks. Starting from Marlay Park in Dublin, the trail stretches over 130 kilometers southward, culminating in the village of Clonegal. Along the way, it weaves through the Wicklow Mountains, offering hikers a variety of landscapes that are as challenging as they are beautiful. One of the most notable sections is the ascent to Djouce Mountain, which provides panoramic views of the Powerscourt Waterfall — Ireland's highest waterfall — and the lush, rolling hills that typify the region. As you continue, the trail brings you to Glendalough, a glacial valley renowned for its early medieval monastic settlement. The ancient ruins, including a round tower and several churches, set against the backdrop of two tranquil lakes, create a palpable sense of walking through history. Further south, the trail meanders through the remote and wild Glenmalure Valley, offering a sense of solitude and grandeur that is rare and invigorating. Each step along the Wicklow Way unveils natural wonders and historical gems, making every mile a discovery.

Preparation Tips

To fully enjoy the Wicklow Way, proper preparation is key. The weather in Ireland can be unpredictable, with possible rain showers even on sunny days, so waterproof gear is essential. A sturdy pair of hiking boots will serve you well on the varied terrains, from muddy paths to rocky inclines. Packing layers is also advisable, as temperatures can change quickly, especially at higher elevations. For navigation, while the Wicklow Way is well-marked with yellow man signs, carrying a detailed map and a compass, or a GPS device, can enhance your experience and ensure you stay on the right path. It's also wise to plan your stops; whether you prefer quaint B&Bs or well-equipped campgrounds, knowing where you'll rest each night frees you to enjoy the day's adventures. Lastly, a basic first-aid kit is crucial for addressing minor injuries on the trail, ensuring that small setbacks don't lead to bigger issues.

Local Flora and Fauna

The biodiversity of the Wicklow Mountains is a highlight for nature enthusiasts. The area is home to a variety of ecosystems, from woodlands to peat bogs, each supporting different species. As you hike, keep an eye out for the native red deer and the elusive Irish hare, especially during the quieter hours of dawn and dusk. Birdwatchers will appreciate the variety of birdlife, including the peregrine falcon, known for its breathtaking speed and agility. The woodlands are filled with the scent of pine and the sights of diverse plant species, including the delicate bog cotton and the hearty gorse, whose yellow flowers brighten the landscape. In spring and early summer, the hillsides bloom with wildflowers, including the striking bluebells that form a carpet under the canopy of trees. This rich tapestry of flora and fauna not only adds to the scenic beauty of the hike but also offers a tranquil escape into nature's embrace.

Cultural Stops

The Wicklow Way is not just a journey through nature, but also a path steeped in Irish culture. Beyond Glendalough's spiritual heritage, the trail offers numerous opportunities to delve into the local culture. Small villages along the route, such as Enniskerry and Roundwood, provide cozy spots for rest and refreshment. Here, you can savor traditional Irish cuisine, perhaps enjoying a hearty stew or freshly baked scones at a local café. These villages also offer a chance to explore local crafts at artisan shops, where hand-knitted woolens or handcrafted jewelry make for unique souvenirs. Additionally, for those interested in the art of whiskey-making, a detour to the Powerscourt Distillery reveals the process behind crafting one of Ireland's most beloved spirits. Each cultural stop adds a layer of richness to your hike, connecting you to the people and traditions that make this region vibrant and welcoming.

Each step on the Wicklow Way offers more than just a walk; it's a journey through the heart of Ireland's natural and cultural land-scapes. As you traverse this path, you are not merely a visitor but a participant in a story that continues to unfold with each mile, each vista, and each encounter.

Kayaking Under the Stars: Bioluminescence in West Cork

Imagine paddling through the calm waters of West Cork at night, the strokes of your kayak disturbing the water and setting off a glow that mirrors the starry sky above. This magical phenomenon, known as bioluminescence, occurs when microorganisms in the water, called dinoflagellates, are agitated by movement. These tiny creatures emit light as a defense mechanism, creating a brilliant natural light show in the waters. The conditions in West Cork are particularly conducive to this spectacle, especially during the warmer months when the water temperatures are higher and the nights are darker. The secluded bays and inlets of this region, away from the light pollution of major cities, offer an ideal backdrop for the bioluminescent display, turning a simple night on the water into an enchanting experience. As you glide through these radiant waters, each paddle stroke ignites a burst of light, surrounding your kayak with what looks like liquid stars, a truly surreal and unforgettable way to engage with nature's wonders.

Ensuring safety while kayaking at night, especially to witness the ethereal beauty of bioluminescence, requires careful preparation and adherence to specific guidelines. Firstly, it is imperative to use a kayak that is stable and suitable for night use, equipped with all necessary safety gear, including life vests, whistles, and waterproof lights. Navigation can be more challenging in the dark, so a reliable GPS device or a compass is essential, as well as familiarity with the area's geography. Opting for a guided tour can enhance the experience, as local guides are not only familiar with the navigational aspects but also skilled in locating the best spots for witnessing bioluminescence. They also ensure adherence to safety protocols, which is crucial when kayaking in potentially unfamiliar waters under low visibility conditions. Additionally, checking weather conditions before setting out is vital, as clear, calm nights provide the best conditions for both safety and for observing the bioluminescence. By preparing adequately and prioritizing safety, you can fully immerse yourself in the mesmerizing beauty of bioluminescent kayaking without undue risk.

The preservation of natural wonders like bioluminescence in West Cork calls for a commitment to eco-tourism principles that ensure minimal impact on the environment. As visitors marvel at the glow of the waters, it becomes crucial to engage in practices that do not disturb the delicate balance of the ecosystem. This includes avoiding the use of chemicals or pollutants near the water bodies, minimizing noise pollution, and following all local guidelines regarding wildlife and habitat protection. The use of eco-friendly equipment, such as solar-powered lights or biodegradable materials, also plays a role in reducing the ecological footprint of night kayaking adventures. Furthermore, participating in or supporting conservation initiatives that protect marine life and promote water cleanliness can contribute to the sustainability of bioluminescence phenomena. By respecting these practices, you help ensure that future generations can also experience the magic of glowing waters, which enhances the appeal of night kayaking and fosters a broader appreciation and respect for nature's marvels.

In addition to the allure of bioluminescence, the area offers a plethora of nocturnal activities that can complement your kayaking adventure. Stargazing, for instance, is particularly rewarding in West Cork, where the dark skies, free from urban light pollution, reveal constellations and celestial events with stunning clarity. Local astronomy clubs often host night sky viewings, providing telescopes and expert insights into the cosmos.

For wildlife enthusiasts, nocturnal walks through the coastal trails can be thrilling, as they present opportunities to observe the habits of nighttime creatures like owls, bats, and foxes. These guided walks are educational and also affords a chance to appreciate the sounds and sights of the Irish countryside after dark. Together, these activities enrich the nighttime experience in West Cork, making it a comprehensive adventure that combines the wonders of the water, sky, and land.

The Cliffs of Moher: Off the Beaten Track

Exploring the Cliffs of Moher often conjures images of standing atop the bustling main viewing platforms, where crowds gather to capture the quintessential shot of these iconic sea cliffs. However, there exists a myriad of less-trodden paths that offer serene and unique vantage points, allowing for a more personal and reflective experience of the cliffs' grandeur. One such path leads to Hag's Head, the southernmost point of the cliffs, which provides a dramatic view of the cliffs curving northward towards O'Brien's Tower. This quieter trail meanders along the cliff edge, offering a peaceful hike where the sounds of the ocean and the calls of seabirds fill the air. Another alternative is the walk from Doolin to the Cliffs, which not only affords spectacular views from a different angle but also traverses lush green fields and traditional stone walls, showcasing the rural beauty that characterizes much of the Irish landscape. These alternative routes are cherished by those who seek to connect with nature away from the crowds, providing moments of solitude and contemplation amidst the awe-inspiring scenery.

Preserving the natural beauty of the Cliffs of Moher is a priority, not only for the sake of environmental conservation but also to maintain the integrity of the visitor experience. The efforts to protect this majestic landscape are evident through the sustainable practices implemented at the site. The visitor center, built into the hillside, is designed to minimize visual impact and houses exhibits that educate visitors on the ecological significance of the cliffs. Conservation initiatives also include restrictions on access to certain areas to prevent erosion and protect nesting sites for seabirds such as puffins, razorbills, and guillemots. Visitors can contribute to these efforts by adhering to marked paths, refraining from littering, and using the shuttle services provided to reduce traffic and pollution. Additionally, supporting local conservation groups or participating in guided eco-tours can enhance understanding of the cliffs' ecology and the importance of preserving such landscapes for future generations.

The Cliffs of Moher are not only a natural wonder but also a canvas of cultural heritage, painted with the tales and legends that have been passed down through generations in County Clare.

One of the most enchanting tales is that of the Mermaid of Moher, who is said to emerge from the depths of the Atlantic and sit atop the cliffs combing her hair with a golden comb. Another legend tells of Mal, a witch who chased after Cormac, a local chieftain she had fallen in love with, across Ireland. The chase ended at the cliffs where Mal jumped to her death, and the spot where she fell was named Hag's Head, in her memory. These stories add a mystical dimension to the cliffs, enriching the visitor experience with a sense of wonder and legacy that goes beyond the visual spectacle. Engaging with these legends through local storytelling sessions or interpretive signs along the trails can provide a deeper, more connected experience of the cliffs as a place of both natural beauty and mythic lore.

Capturing the majestic beauty of the Cliffs of Moher through photography is a pursuit that beckons countless visitors each year. For those looking to photograph the cliffs, timing and perspective are key. The soft light of early morning or late afternoon can dramatically enhance the textures and colors of the cliffs, casting long shadows and illuminating the lush greenery and ocean with a golden hue. The variability of the Irish weather can also provide dramatic backdrops, with rolling clouds or mist creating ethereal and powerful images. Photographers willing to explore different angles and settings can find unique compositions, such as capturing the reflection of the cliffs in the puddles left by the receding tide or framing the cliffs with wildflowers in the foreground. Remembering to respect the natural environment while seeking out the best shots will ensure that the beauty of the Cliffs of Moher continues to inspire awe and wonder for all who visit.

Cycling the Greenways: Mayo's Great Western Trail

The Great Western Greenway, stretching an impressive 42 kilometers from the bustling town of Westport to the tranquil Achill Sound in County Mayo, offers a spectacular route for cyclists of all levels to immerse themselves in the raw beauty of the Irish countryside. As you pedal along this path, which follows the route of the historic Midland Great Western Railway, you are treated to a visual feast of coastal views, mountain ranges, and verdant landscapes. Notable stops along the way include the picturesque town of Newport, with its beautiful viaduct and the serene shores of Clew Bay, where the silhouette of Croagh Patrick adds a mystical backdrop. Further along, Mulranny offers a gateway to unspoiled beaches and salt marshes, providing an ideal spot for a restful break. The trail culminates in Achill, where the rugged cliffs and expansive Atlantic views are truly breathtaking. Each segment of the Greenway promises a unique scenic experience, inviting you to slow down and appreciate the stunning vistas that unfold with each turn of the pedal.

In the charming town of Westport, several bike rental shops cater to visitors eager to explore the Greenway. Clew Bay Bike Hire, for instance, offers a range of bicycles suitable for different ages and abilities, from robust mountain bikes to comfortable hybrids, ensuring that every rider finds the perfect fit for their adventure. They also provide all the necessary gear, including helmets, high-visibility jackets, and detailed maps of the trail. For those looking for a guided experience, many shops offer the option of organized tours, which can enhance the journey with insights into the local history and geography. Additionally, these shops typically offer a shuttle service back from Achill to Westport, allowing you to enjoy the trail at your own pace without worrying about the return journey. Whether you choose to go it alone or with a guided group, the available amenities and support make cycling the Greenway a smooth and enjoyable experience.

The Great Western Greenway not only connects landscapes but also cultures. Along the route, opportunities abound to engage with the local heritage, from traditional Irish music sessions in snug pubs to craft workshops where local artisans share their skills. In Newport, the Grainne Uaile Heritage Centre offers a glimpse into the area's rich history, often complemented by impromptu traditional music performances that enrich the cultural experience. Mulranny, known for its vibrant arts scene, hosts several workshops where you can try your hand at every-thing from pottery to seaweed foraging, activities that connect you with traditional crafts and local natural resources. These cultural encounters provide a more profound connection to the regions you cycle through, turning the Greenway into a corridor of cultural discovery where every pedal brings you closer to the heart of Irish heritage.

As for dining, the towns and villages along the Greenway boast numerous eateries that showcase the best of Mayo's local produce. In Westport, The Pantry & Corkscrew offers dishes crafted from locally sourced ingredients, serving up a taste of the region in every bite. For those on the move, The Greenway Café in Newport provides the perfect pit stop, with delicious homemade cakes and a hearty cyclist's breakfast that offers a much-needed energy boost. Mulranny's Gourmet Greenway is an initiative that highlights local artisan food producers, and many cafes and restaurants participate, giving you a taste of specialties such as Achill Island sea salt and Clew Bay scallops. Picnic spots abound along the route, with breathtaking views that complement a simple, fresh meal. Whether you choose to dine in a cozy café or picnic under the open sky, the local gastronomy adds a delightful flavor to your cycling adventure, making every meal a memorable part of your Greenway experience.

Birdwatching in the Wilds of Donegal

In the rugged landscapes of Donegal, birdwatching transforms into an exhilarating pursuit, where the diversity of avian life reflects the unspoiled beauty of this region. From the majestic golden eagles soaring high above the Glenveagh National Park to the charming puffins nesting on the cliffs of Horn Head, Donegal offers a birdwatching experience as varied and vibrant as its landscapes. The coastal areas teem with seabirds like gannets and kittiwakes, their calls a wild chorus that accompanies the crash of the Atlantic waves. Inland, the boglands and woodlands provide refuge for species such as the elusive corncrake and the vibrant kingfisher, each species adding a unique note to the symphony of bird calls that fill the air. Whether you are a seasoned ornithologist or a casual observer, the feathered inhabitants of Donegal provide a fascinating window into the interplay of ecology and geography in one of Ireland's most scenic counties.

For those keen to explore Donegal's rich birdlife, timing and location are key. The cliffs and islands along the coast, such as those at Malin Head, Ireland's northernmost point, offer spectacular views of nesting seabirds, especially during the breeding season from April to July. Here, the cliffs thrum with the activity of thousands of seabirds, providing an unforgettable spectacle of nature in its most raw and beautiful form. Moving inland, the Glenveagh National Park is not just famous for its stunning scenery but also as a haven for birds of prey, including the rare golden eagle, reintroduced to Ireland in the early 2000s. The best times to visit are during the early hours of the morning or later in the evening when the birds are most active. For those interested in migratory patterns, the autumn months offer a chance to observe species like the Brent Goose and the Whooper Swan, as they stop over in Donegal's wetlands during their arduous journey south.

Conservation efforts in Donegal are crucial in maintaining the delicate balance of its ecosystems, which support such a rich variety of bird species. Initiatives such as the EU LIFE project work towards preserving habitats for the corncrake, one of Europe's most threatened farmland birds, which finds refuge in the hay meadows of Donegal. Local conservation groups also engage in habitat management projects, such as maintaining heathlands and wetlands, which are vital for species like the red grouse and the curlew. These efforts help protect these birds and ensure the conservation of the natural heritage of the region, promoting biodiversity and resilience in the face of environmental changes. Visitors are encouraged to respect these efforts by adhering to guidelines such as sticking to marked trails and avoiding disturbance to nesting sites, ensuring their birdwatching adventures support the ongoing preservation of Donegal's natural beauty.

For a more structured exploration of Donegal's birdwatching opportunities, guided tours can offer an enriched experience. These tours, often led by local experts, provide insights into the habits and habitats of various species, enhancing your understanding and appreciation of the birds you encounter. Whether it's a guided walk through the dunes of Magheraroarty, where you can spot breeding lapwings and skylarks, or a boat trip to Tory Island, where colonies of puffins and razorbills nest, these tours can tailor your experience to your interests and provide a deeper, more informed engagement with Donegal's birdlife. Additionally, many guides are actively involved in conservation work and can offer a firsthand look at the efforts to protect these species and their habitats, making your birdwatching experience not just enjoyable but also educational.

Wildflower Walks: The Biodiversity of The Burren

In the heart of County Clare lies The Burren, a unique karst landscape renowned for its remarkable floral diversity and striking geological formations. This rocky terrain, characterized by vast limestone pavements with crisscrossing cracks known as "grikes," forms a distinctive ecosystem where Arctic, Mediterranean, and Alpine plants coexist unusually side by side. The secret to this floral diversity lies in the region's unique climatic and geological conditions. The limestone, with its high pH levels, acts as a natural reservoir, storing warmth and moisture that allow for the survival of a wide variety of plant species typically not found together in such proximity. As you stroll through The Burren, the landscape unveils a botanical mosaic where delicate mountain avens mingle with robust orchids, and the rare maidenhair fern nestles next to the wind-toughened shrubs.

Timing your visit to The Burren can greatly enhance the experience, as the landscape transforms with the seasons, each offering a new palette of colors and species. Spring arrives with a burst of life, as the first purple orchids and gentians bloom, dotting the grey limestone with splashes of color. This season offers a fresh beauty, with early flowers emerging from the rocks, defying the harsh conditions. As the year progresses into summer, the floral display reaches its peak. The Burren becomes a carpet of wildflowers, including the iconic blue gentian and the vivacious yellow bird's-foot trefoil. Walking through these fields during the late spring and early summer months, you are treated to a vibrant spectacle of biodiversity, with each step revealing different species thriving in this calcareous substrate.

To truly appreciate the ecological complexity and conservation significance of The Burren, guided nature walks led by local botanists or conservationists provide invaluable insights. These experts, deeply familiar with the region's ecology, offer detailed explanations of the adaptive strategies of the flora and the conservation efforts in place to protect this unique landscape. They can point out easily overlooked species, share stories of the area's natural history, and discuss ongoing research and protection strategies. Many of these walks also focus on the symbiotic relationships between the plants and their environment, highlighting how such a diverse range of species has adapted to the unique conditions of The Burren. For those passionate about conservation, these guided tours educate and inspire, emphasizing the delicate balance of ecosystems and the importance of efforts to preserve such natural heritages.

As visitors traverse the limestone pavements and marvel at the floral wonders of The Burren, the importance of adhering to eco-friendly practices becomes evident. The survival of this fragile ecosystem depends on the conscientious behavior of its visitors. Sticking to marked trails helps prevent damage to the plant life and reduces soil erosion, preserving the natural habitat for future generations. Additionally, the Leave No Trace principles are encouraged, urging visitors to minimize their impact by taking away all litter and respecting wildlife and plant life. These practices ensure that the biodiversity of The Burren continues to thrive and remain a source of scientific interest and natural beauty. Moreover, by choosing to participate in eco-certified tours and supporting local conservation initiatives, visitors contribute positively to the sustainability of the region, helping to fund projects and raise awareness about the ecological value of The Burren.

As this chapter closes on the serene and stark beauty of The Burren, you carry with you not just memories of its visual splendor and floral diversity but also a deeper understanding of the interconnectedness of nature and the importance of conservation efforts. These themes of natural beauty and ecological responsibility weave through the narratives of Ireland's outdoor escapes, highlighting the country's commitment to preserving its environmental treasures. As we transition from the wild landscapes of The Burren to the next chapter, where the focus shifts to the historical and cultural tapestries that drape the Irish countryside, the journey continues to offer paths that lead through scenic views and also through the rich stories and heritage of Ireland.

CHAPTER 4

MASTERING IRISH WEATHER: PACKING AND PREP

I magine the gentle mist of an early Irish morning caressing your face as you step out into the lush landscape, where every hue of green seems to hold a droplet of dew. The weather in Ireland, a character in its own right, shapes not just the land but also the daily adventures of those who traverse its rolling hills and charming streets. This chapter is your guide to embracing the whimsical Irish weather, ensuring you are well-prepared to enjoy every experience, come rain or shine. From the soft showers of spring to the crisp breezes of autumn, understanding what to pack and how to prepare can transform your journey from a mere visit to a delightful immersion in all things Irish.

Packing for Ireland: A Seasonal Guide

Spring Showers to Summer Sunshine

As you plan your journey to Ireland, envision the months from March to May, where spring showers are as frequent as the blooming daffodils. Packing a lightweight, waterproof rain jacket becomes essential, as it allows you to explore the likes of Dublin's cobbled lanes or the Cliffs of Moher without the rain dampening your spirits. As the calendar turns to summer, especially from June to August, the weather often warms, but the breeze off the Atlantic can bring cooler evenings. This necessitates layers that you can easily add or remove—think breathable fabrics like cotton or linen paired with a warm sweater for those chillier nights spent enjoying live music in a bustling pub.

During these months, an umbrella is a must-have, small enough to tuck into your daypack, yet sturdy enough to withstand a gusty Irish gale. Also, consider packable rain gear; a foldable raincoat or poncho can be a lifesaver during unexpected downpours and takes up minimal space in your luggage. This adaptability in your attire will ensure that whether you're catching the first rays of sun at Bray Head or wandering through the historical ruins of Glendalough, you're comfortably attired and ready for Ireland's capricious skies.

Autumn Winds to Winter Chills

Transitioning into the months of September through November, the crisp air of autumn sweeps across Ireland, carrying with it a palette of rich golds and reds in the foliage. This season, along with winter, from December to February, requires more substantial gear. Waterproof footwear is non-negotiable, ideally with a good grip for those damp, leaf-strewn paths or frosty morning walks along the River Liffey. Investing in thermal layers—merino wool or thermal synthetics—is wise, as they provide insulation without bulk, perfect for layering under a waterproof outer shell.

Scarves, gloves, and a warm hat should also find a place in your suitcase, protecting against the biting winds that often accompany both seasons. These accessories will add a touch of Irish flair to your ensemble, especially if you choose items crafted from traditional Irish wool. As you wander through winter markets or enjoy the rugged, stark beauty of the Irish coast under a gray, brooding sky, these layers will keep you toasty and ensure your focus remains on the enchantment of Ireland, not the cold.

All-Weather Must-Haves

Regardless of when you visit, some items are indispensable for any season in Ireland. A versatile, waterproof jacket is your best friend, capable of shielding you from sudden showers while also serving as a windbreaker on gustier days. Similarly, an umbrella should be a constant companion, lightweight and collapsible, yet durable enough to handle the occasional wild Irish rainstorm. These essentials ensure that, no matter the weather, you are prepared to step out and soak in the lush Irish landscapes and vibrant city scenes without hesitation.

Light and Packable Solutions

Optimizing luggage space while being prepared for all weather conditions is a skill, and with the right choices, you can master this art. Packable rain jackets and travel-sized umbrellas are perfect for saving space yet providing the necessary protection against Irish weather. Layering options that fold compactly, like fleece liners or lightweight down jackets, offer warmth when needed and tuck away discreetly when not. This approach keeps your travel bag light and prepares you for the full range of Ireland's weather patterns, allowing you to embrace every rain-soaked or sunlit moment of your Irish adventure.

As you prepare your wardrobe for Ireland, remember that the key is versatility and adaptability—qualities that mirror the Irish climate itself. With the right gear, every rain-drenched pathway or sunlit hill becomes a part of your unforgettable journey through the Emerald Isle, each weathered moment adding depth and joy to your exploration of this enchanting country.

Embracing the Elements: Outdoor Gear Essentials

Navigating the landscapes of Ireland, where the elements can change as swiftly as the folklore tales spun in its ancient pubs, demands not just spirit but also the right gear. Understanding the distinction between waterproof and water-resistant items is essential in a land known for its frequent drizzles and downpours. Waterproof gear, rigorously tested to withstand penetration by water, is indispensable for those inevitable days when Irish rains seek to envelop the countryside. Such gear employs membranes or coatings that block water on a molecular level, ideal for prolonged exposure to wet conditions. Water-resistant items, while offering a degree of protection, are typically suited for light rain and brief encounters with moisture. These are treated with a coating that repels water, but under persistent rain, their efficacy wanes. As you prepare to traverse the verdant hills or explore the rugged coastlines, opting for truly waterproof jackets and trousers ensures that the rain enriches the experience rather than dampens it.

Footwear, the steadfast companion on any trail, must be chosen with care and consideration of Ireland's diverse terrain. For those venturing into the rural landscapes, where trails can range from soft earth padded with moss to rocky outcrops slick with rain, durable waterproof hiking boots are the order of the day. These boots offer protection from water and support for the ankles, crucial when navigating uneven ground. For city explorers, where ancient cobblestones and modern pavements create a mosaic underfoot, waterproof walking shoes offer a blend of comfort and protection, ensuring that a day exploring the likes of Dublin or Galway is marked by enjoyment, not discomfort. In both cases, the key lies in footwear that marries robust functionality with comfort, ensuring that each step taken across Ireland's storied landscapes is one of assured ease.

When the wild winds sweep across the cliffs and through the valleys, windproof accessories become not just additions but necessities. A good quality, windproof hat and a scarf can transform a blustery day from a battle against the elements to a bracing encounter with the raw beauty of Ireland. Hats should cover the ears and stay snug against gusts that sweep off the Atlantic, while scarves should be of a material thick enough to block the wind yet soft enough to prevent chafing as you turn your face to the ocean winds. These accessories serve a practical purpose and add an element of style to your outdoor attire, reflecting the rustic chic that is as much a part of Ireland as its weather.

Lastly, the choice of backpacks and bags must reflect an understanding of the need to shield your essentials from the rain. Water-resistant backpacks, crafted with materials that repel water, are vital for protecting items like cameras, maps, and snacks. Look for bags with sealed or covered zippers and compartments, ensuring that even in a downpour, your belongings remain dry. For those who carry electronics, whether for capturing memories or navigating through the Irish countryside, ensuring these are safeguarded against the rain is paramount. A bag with a built-in rain cover, or even a separate rain cover that can be slipped over the bag during a shower, offers an added layer of security against the elements, allowing you to embrace the Irish weather in all its moods without reservation.

Staying Dry and Stylish: Fashion Tips for the Irish Climate

Navigating the ever-changing weather of Ireland calls for a wardrobe that is as versatile as it is stylish. When it comes to layering like a local, the secret lies in choosing fabrics that provide warmth and allow your skin to breathe, adapting comfortably to both indoor warmth and outdoor chill. Merino wool, renowned for its exceptional thermal regulation properties, makes an excellent base layer. Unlike traditional wool, merino is exceptionally soft and manages moisture better than most fabrics, keeping you dry and comfortable as you explore bustling markets or serene trails. Over this, layer a breathable fleece or a lightweight down jacket for insulation, and top it off with a chic, waterproof outer shell. This layering technique ensures you stay warm without overheating, and the ease of adding or removing layers allows you to respond swiftly to the whims of Irish weather.

The casual yet chic fashion sense in Ireland blends practicality with a touch of effortless style, making it easy to blend in with the locals. Irish wardrobes often feature staples like well-fitted jeans or trousers paired with layered tops and a classic, tailored coat. For women, a long cardigan or a casual blazer can be paired with a scarf—perhaps one made from local Donegal tweed for that authentic Irish flair. Men might opt for a lambswool sweater under a waxed cotton jacket, which is not only stylish but also water-resistant. These pieces are not just about looking good; they're about practicality and comfort, suitable for a country where you might experience all four seasons in one day.

When it comes to staying dry, your choice of raincoat can make all the difference. Brands like Stutterheim or Hunter offer raincoats that promise to keep you dry without sacrificing style. These raincoats come in a variety of colors and cuts, ensuring that they shield you from the rain while complementing your outfit. For accessories, consider a waterproof leather bag or a treated canvas backpack. These materials not only resist water but also age beautifully, gaining character with each raindrop they weather. Pair these with a stylish umbrella—perhaps one with a print of classic Irish symbols or landscapes—and you're ready to face the Irish drizzle with style.

Footwear in Ireland must be sturdy yet stylish, capable of handling a sudden downpour or a leisurely stroll through an ancient castle's rocky grounds. Brands like Blundstone or Dubarry provide boots that are both fashionable and functional, crafted to handle the diverse terrain of Ireland. These boots often feature water-resistant leather and durable soles designed for grip and comfort, perfect for navigating both the urban cobblestones and the countryside's uneven paths. For a more urban setting, water-proof leather sneakers or rubber-soled boots offer a chic, practical choice, keeping your feet dry and comfortable without compromising on style. By choosing the right footwear, you ensure that every step you take across Ireland's varied landscapes is a blend of comfort, protection, and style, allowing you to enjoy the beauty and heritage of this enchanting land without a worry about the weather.

Tech Prep: Gadgets for Capturing Ireland's Beauty

Navigating the verdant landscapes and historic cobblestone streets of Ireland, you'll likely want to capture the myriad of moments that present themselves, from the misty mornings over the Cliffs of Moher to the vibrant nightlife of Dublin. Equipping yourself with the right camera gear and ensuring its protection against Ireland's often damp conditions is crucial. A DSLR or mirrorless camera with a weather-sealed body is ideal, offering resilience against the elements while providing high-quality images. Lenses should also be chosen with versatility and environmental conditions in mind; a good standard zoom lens can cover most situations, though a weather-sealed lens is a bonus. For those inevitable drizzles or the occasional downpour, a waterproof camera cover is indispensable. It's lightweight, easy to pack, and ensures your gear remains dry, allowing you to continue shooting even when the weather turns. Additionally, consider a sturdy, lightweight tripod that can stand firm against Ireland's gusty winds, essential for those wanting to capture the rugged landscapes in all their long-exposure glory.

Power solutions while traveling in Ireland must address the practicalities of a full day's exploration. Portable chargers are a traveler's best friend, providing the juice needed for smartphones, cameras, and other electronic devices on the go. Look for a high-capacity power bank that can offer multiple charges in a single day, ensuring you're never caught off guard when your battery dips. Equally important is a universal travel adapter compatible with Ireland's socket type. This small, often overlooked accessory is vital, allowing you to recharge your devices in any standard Irish outlet, ensuring you start each day fully charged and ready to capture every adventure that comes your way.

When it comes to staying ahead of Ireland's unpredictable weather, a good weather app is your digital oracle. Apps like AccuWeather or the Weather Channel provide real-time forecasts with radar imaging, perfect for planning your outings around rain showers or for seizing those sunny intervals for a trip to the coastal towns. These apps often offer hourly weather updates, which can be incredibly handy for photographers looking to capture the perfect sunrise or sunset, or hikers trying to gauge the best time to hit the trails. Adapting your plans based on the weather enriches your experience and prevents Ireland's unpredictable climate from disrupting your itinerary.

For those venturing into the more remote parts of Ireland, where cell service can be spotty, having reliable navigation tools is essential. A robust GPS device is recommended for anyone planning to explore Ireland's extensive network of rural roads and pathways. Devices specifically designed for hiking or driving come preloaded with maps that can be a lifeline in areas where mobile signals fail. For added backup, consider downloading offline maps onto your smartphone or tablet through apps like Google Maps or Maps.me, which offer detailed, navigable maps without the need for an internet connection. These tools guide you through unfamiliar terrain and enrich your experience, allowing you to delve deeper into Ireland's breathtaking landscapes with confidence and ease, making every moment countable and every path worth exploring.

Rainy Day Delights: Enjoying Ireland Indoors

When the Irish skies decide to grace the day with rain, an opportunity unfolds to explore the cultural heartbeats pulsating within the walls of Ireland's museums and galleries. These sanctuaries of art and history offer a perfect refuge, combining the warmth of shelter with the richness of Irish heritage. The National Gallery in Dublin, with its vast collection of Irish and European art, provides an aesthetic feast that can easily consume hours of attentive exploration. Here, masterpieces by Jack B. Yeats, brother of the famous poet W.B. Yeats, share space with works by Vermeer and Picasso, offering diverse perspectives under one roof. For those with a penchant for modern art, the Irish Museum of Modern Art, housed in the historic Royal Hospital Kilmainham, presents cutting-edge exhibitions and installations that provoke thought and stir the emotions. These cultural excursions not only shelter you from the rain but also immerse you in the narratives and beauty that have shaped Irish identity across the centuries.

Stepping into a traditional Irish pub offers another delightful escape from the rain, where the warm glow of the fire and the rich timbre of live folk music create an enveloping atmosphere of coziness and camaraderie. The Brazen Head, Dublin's oldest pub, dating back to 1198, is a treasure trove of historical anecdotes and traditional Irish music, offering a direct line to the past over a pint of stout or a hot toddy. As the music plays and the fire crackles, conversations flow freely, spinning threads of new friendships or deepening old ones. These pubs are not just places to drink; they are the living rooms of their communities, where warmth is shared physically and metaphorically, and the weather outside becomes a mere backdrop to the richness of interaction inside.

For those who prefer active indoor adventures, Ireland's options abound. The Titanic Belfast, an interactive museum located at the site of the famed ship's construction, offers a poignant journey through the Titanic's story, from conception to tragic demise. For a more physically engaging experience, indoor climbing centers like Awesome Walls in Dublin provide challenges for all skill levels, with expert instructors to guide you. These venues offer a way to stretch your limbs and challenge your body while the landscape outside is draped in rain. Whiskey tastings, another excellent indoor pursuit, can be enjoyed at one of the many distilleries like Jameson Distillery Bow St. in Dublin. Here, guided tours reveal the secrets of whiskey-making followed by tastings that warm the throat and spirit, proving that a rainy day in Ireland can be as enriching as any spent under the sun.

For relaxation and rejuvenation, the array of Irish spas and wellness centers offer a sanctuary where the therapeutic touch of skilled practitioners promises to melt away any residual chill from the rain-soaked outdoors. The seaweed baths at Voya Seaweed Baths in Sligo, for instance, use locally harvested seaweed to detoxify the body and enrich the skin with essential minerals, a practice rooted in Irish tradition but perfect for the modern traveler seeking relaxation. Alternatively, luxurious spas like the Europe Hotel & Resort in Killarney provide thermal suites and hydrotherapy that utilize the healing properties of water in various forms, from steam to ice, ensuring that your indoor day revitalizes every part of you. These wellness experiences provide a perfect counterpoint to the brisk outdoor adventures, proving that every aspect of Irish weather can be matched with a fittingly delightful indoor activity.

Health and Safety: Navigating Ireland with Peace of Mind

Traveling to Ireland, with its captivating landscapes and vibrant city scenes, is an adventure that calls for careful preparation, particularly when it comes to ensuring your health and safety. The importance of securing comprehensive travel insurance cannot be overstated. This type of insurance is your safety net, covering everything from medical emergencies and hospital stays to lost luggage and trip cancellations. Before you embark, make sure your policy covers the full duration of your stay and any specific activities you plan to engage in, such as hiking or cycling, ensuring that you're protected no matter what comes your way. It's not just about having coverage; it's about having peace of mind, allowing you to fully immerse yourself in the Irish experience without undue worry about potential mishaps.

When it comes to health care and emergency services, Ireland is well-equipped to assist should the need arise. Familiarizing yourself with the basics of accessing these services can make all the difference in urgent situations. In Ireland, the number to dial for emergency services is 112 or 999. These numbers connect you to the ambulance, fire brigade, and police, ensuring rapid response for any medical or safety issues. For less urgent health concerns, local pharmacies are an excellent resource. Pharmacists in Ireland can offer medical advice and treatment for minor ailments, such as colds or allergies, and can direct you to a doctor if more specialized care is needed. Remember, it's advisable to carry a small first aid kit with you for minor cuts or scrapes, especially if you're venturing into the countryside or engaging in outdoor activities.

Speaking of the great outdoors, Ireland's landscapes are as inviting as they are rugged, making safety in these environments a priority. When hiking in areas like the Wicklow Mountains or along the coastal cliffs, it's crucial to stick to marked trails. These paths not only guide you through the most scenic routes but also ensure you're traversing areas that have been assessed for safety. Always check the weather forecast before heading out; conditions in Ireland can change rapidly, and what starts as a sunny morning can quickly turn into a foggy afternoon. Adequate preparation includes dressing in layers, carrying waterproof gear, and informing someone of your itinerary. Moreover, understanding the signs of hypothermia and knowing how to react if someone starts showing symptoms is vital during colder months or when hiking at higher elevations.

Urban exploration in Ireland is as thrilling as its rural adventures, though it comes with its own set of safety considerations. Cities like Dublin, Cork, and Galway are generally safe, but, as with any major city, it pays to be cautious, especially at night. Stick to well-lit, populated areas and be mindful of your belongings in crowded spots such as markets, festivals, or public transport, where pick-pockets could be a risk. If you're enjoying Ireland's renowned nightlife, keep an eye on your drinks and travel in groups when possible. It's also wise to have a plan for getting back to your accommodation safely, whether that means keeping the number of a reputable taxi service on hand or using public transport before service ends for the night.

Navigating the health and safety landscape of Ireland with aware-ness and preparedness allows you to embrace all the joys and discoveries of your visit while minimizing potential risks. This approach ensures a smoother trip and enriches your travel experi-ence, leaving you free to create lasting memories across the Emerald Isle.

Wrapping Up the Essentials

This chapter has equipped you with the essentials for mastering Irish weather and ensuring your health and safety, setting the stage for a journey filled with confidence and enjoyment. You're now ready to step into Ireland's ever-changing landscapes and vibrant cultural scenes, armed with the knowledge to embrace every experience, rain or shine, city street or mountain trail. As we transition from the practical preparations to the historical and cultural explorations in the next chapter, your adventure continues to unfold, enriched by the assurance that you are well-prepared to navigate whatever comes your way.

CHAPTER 5
NAVIGATING IRELAND: TRANSPORTATION SIMPLIFIED

As you contemplate the rolling hills and vast stretches of coastline that define the Irish landscape, imagine the freedom of exploring this stunning terrain at your own pace, stopping where and when you wish. The independence to veer off the main roads into the heart of Ireland's picturesque villages and secluded natural wonders is a compelling reason to consider renting a car. This chapter is designed to guide you through the nuances of car hire in Ireland, ensuring you are well-equipped to navigate the charming yet sometimes challenging Irish roads.

To Rent or Not to Rent: A Car Hire Guide

Navigating Rural Ireland

Renting a car in Ireland opens up a treasure trove of opportunities for the intrepid explorer. The country's rural beauty, from the wilds of Connemara to the rugged peninsulas of Kerry, is often best experienced at a leisurely pace, accessible primarily by car. Unlike more urban destinations where attractions are concentrated, Ireland's magic lies scattered across its landscape. By renting a car, you gain the flexibility to explore ancient stone circles, hidden beaches, and remote pubs that public transport simply cannot reach. Imagine driving along the scenic Ring of Kerry, with the freedom to stop for an impromptu photo session beside a cascading waterfall or to enjoy a spontaneous hike up a secluded trail. The convenience of a car allows you to discover these off-the-beaten-path gems at your own rhythm, making every turn an adventure and every vista a memory.

Understanding Insurance and Fees

Navigating the intricacies of car rental insurance and associated fees in Ireland is crucial to avoid unexpected costs and ensure a smooth experience. Standard car rental insurance in Ireland typically includes a Collision Damage Waiver (CDW) and theft protection, which limits your financial liability in case of damage or theft of the vehicle. However, it's important to understand that CDW usually comes with a deductible, which can be quite high. To reduce this deductible to zero, or close to it, you can opt for Excess Waiver Insurance, offered at an additional daily fee. Be wary of additional fees that may not be immediately apparent, such as charges for additional drivers, GPS devices, or car seats. Always read the rental agreement carefully and ask for clarification on any charges that are not clear. This will help you budget accurately and avoid the stress of unforeseen expenses, allowing you to focus on enjoying the drive and the stunning Irish landscape unfolding before you.

Driving on the Left

For many visitors, particularly those from countries where driving on the right is the norm, adapting to driving on the left side of the road can be daunting. The key to mastering this change lies in giving yourself time to adjust. Consider starting your driving journey in less congested areas, rather than navigating out of a busy airport. Roundabouts, a common feature in Irish roads, can be particularly tricky. Remember to always give way to traffic coming from the right and signal your exit. Practice these new rules in a safe environment if possible. Many car rental companies are attuned to the needs of international drivers and may provide you with a brief orientation or driving tips to help you feel more comfortable before you hit the road.

Eco-Friendly Options

For the environmentally conscious traveler, Ireland offers an increasing number of eco-friendly rental options. Hybrid and electric vehicles (EVs) are available at major rental stations and are a great way to reduce your carbon footprint while exploring the country. While EV charging stations are becoming more widespread across Ireland, planning is essential to ensure that your routes align with charging station locations, particularly in rural areas. Renting a hybrid or electric vehicle not only contributes to preserving Ireland's natural beauty but also aligns with the global shift towards sustainable travel practices. By choosing an eco-friendly car, you are part of a growing community of travelers committed to responsible tourism, ensuring that the lush landscapes of Ireland can be enjoyed by generations to come.

Navigating the roads of Ireland offers a unique blend of freedom, adventure, and responsibility. From understanding the practical aspects of car hire to embracing the challenge of driving on the left, each element of your journey contributes to a richer travel experience. As you cruise along the coastal highways or meander through historic towns, the stories of Ireland unfold at your own pace, guided by your curiosity and secured by your preparations.

This chapter not only equips you with the knowledge to navigate these roads safely and confidently, but also invites you to weave your own path through the enchanting landscapes of Ireland.

Public Transport Pro Tips: Buses and Trains

Navigating Ireland by public transport is an enriching experience that offers convenience and the opportunity to interact with locals and enjoy scenic views without the worry of driving. Ireland's public transport network is robust, encompassing a wide range of bus and train services that connect major cities as well as remote areas. Bus Éireann, the national bus company, provides comprehensive coverage across the country, offering both intercity and local services. For train travel, Iarnród Éireann (Irish Rail) operates routes that link Dublin with other major cities, including Cork, Limerick, Galway, and Belfast, with branch lines reaching out to smaller communities. The convenience of these services makes them an excellent choice for traveling across Ireland, whether you're heading from Dublin's bustling streets to the historic heart of Cork or from the serene landscapes of Connemara to the lively atmosphere of Galway.

For cost-effective travel, understanding the range of ticketing options available can significantly enhance your experience. The Leap Card, an integrated public transport card, offers a cashless way to pay for travel across Dublin's city buses, trams (Luas), and suburban rails. It provides flexibility and savings, with fares typically lower than single-purchase tickets. For tourists, the Leap Visitor Card is particularly useful; available for 1, 3, or 7 days, it allows unlimited travel across the network for the duration it is valid. Outside of Dublin, the 'Open Road' bus pass by Bus Éireann is an excellent option for those planning extensive travel by bus, offering unlimited travel for consecutive days. Train travelers can benefit from the Irish Rail's Explorer Card, which allows unlimited train travel for specified periods. These options can ease your travels and afford significant savings, making exploring Ireland more enjoyable and affordable.

One of the joys of traveling through Ireland by public transport is the chance to witness some of Europe's most stunning landscapes from the comfort of your seat. Train journeys like the route from Dublin to Sligo offer expansive views of the Irish countryside, unveiling a tapestry of rolling fields, ancient castles, and quaint towns. The train ride between Cork and Cobh is another scenic delight, providing picturesque views of Cork Harbour, one of the largest natural harbors in the world. For those who prefer bus travel, the route from Galway to Clifden immerses passengers in the wild beauty of Connemara, with its rugged terrain and dramatic coastline. These journeys not only connect destinations but also turn the travel itself into a memorable part of your Irish adventure, filled with breathtaking vistas that are as captivating as the places you set out to explore.

Ensuring accessibility in public transport is crucial for travelers with disabilities to fully enjoy their visit to Ireland. Both Bus Éireann and Irish Rail are committed to providing accessible services. Most buses are equipped with low-floor entry and designated spaces for wheelchairs, while major train stations offer ramp access and assistance on request. It is advisable to contact the transport providers in advance to arrange any necessary assistance and to confirm accessibility features on specific routes. Additionally, the Transport for Ireland website provides comprehensive information on accessible transport options, helping you plan a smooth and enjoyable travel experience across Ireland. By taking advantage of these services, you ensure that your exploration of Ireland is comfortable and inclusive, allowing you to focus on the beauty and charm of your surroundings.

Biking in Ireland: What You Need to Know

Exploring Ireland on two wheels unveils an entirely different facet of its charm, blending the thrill of discovery with the joy of being outdoors. Whether you're cruising through bustling city streets or pedaling along serene rural paths, biking in Ireland offers a fresh perspective on its landscapes and culture. City bike rental schemes like Dublin's Just Eat, dublinbikes or Cork's Coke Zero Bikes provide an excellent way for visitors to integrate into the urban flow. These services are conveniently located throughout the cities, featuring docking stations where bikes can be picked up and dropped off, making them ideal for short trips around the city centers or leisurely rides along designated bike paths such as those along Dublin's Grand Canal. For those venturing into the countryside, many local bike shops offer rental services where you can hire everything from basic models to high-end road bikes, often providing helpful advice on routes that cater to various interests and skill levels.

Safety while cycling in Ireland is paramount and adhering to local road laws is essential for a secure and enjoyable experience. Helmets, though not legally required for adults, are strongly advised and often come included with your bike rental. Visibility can be a concern, particularly on rural roads or during the unpredictable Irish weather; wearing high-visibility jackets and using bike lights during dusk, dawn, or cloudy days helps ensure you are seen by motorists. The rules of the road in Ireland require cyclists to follow the same regulations as motorists, including signaling turns and obeying traffic lights and signs. Special care should be taken on narrow country roads, which while scenic, can be winding and sometimes host fast-moving local traffic. Cyclists should keep to the left, ride in single file on these narrower roads, and always be mindful of the weather conditions, as rain can make roads slippery and reduce visibility.

The diversity of bike trails in Ireland caters to every type of cyclist, from family-friendly rides to challenging mountain bike adventures. The Great Western Greenway in Mayo offers a splendid route for families and leisure cyclists, with its relatively flat path that stretches 42 kilometers from Westport to Achill, showcasing some of Ireland's most spectacular landscapes. For more seasoned cyclists, the Ballyhoura Mountain Bike Trails in County Limerick present a thrilling challenge with over 90 kilometers of trails, varying in difficulty and offering everything from tight turns and steep climbs to exhilarating downhill sections. Each trail is clearly marked, with detailed maps available at the trailhead, ensuring riders can find a route that matches their ability and adventure level. These trails provide a physical challenge and offer a unique way to engage with the natural environment, often leading to hidden spots that are not accessible by car.

For those who prefer a structured approach to cycling in Ireland, numerous bike touring companies offer guided tours that combine physical activity with cultural exploration. Companies like Irish Cycling Safaris and Go Visit Ireland specialize in cycling tours that take you through some of the most picturesque parts of the country, from the rugged coasts of the Wild Atlantic Way to the historic landmarks of Ireland's Ancient East. These tours often include expert guides who provide insights into the history and culture of the areas you visit, enhancing your ride with stories and facts that deepen your connection to the landscape. Additionally, these companies take care of all logistics, including bike rentals, accommodation, and even meals, making them a fantastic option for those who want to dive deep into Ireland's scenic offerings without the hassle of planning every detail. Whether you're looking to explore Ireland at a leisurely pace or push your limits on challenging terrains, these guided tours offer a memorable and comprehensive biking experience tailored to a variety of interests and skill levels.

Walking Tours: Seeing Ireland at a Slower Pace

Walking through Ireland offers a unique way to connect with its rich history, vibrant culture, and breathtaking landscapes at a pace that allows you to absorb every detail. Guided city walking tours are particularly popular, as they delve into the intricate past and present of Ireland's bustling cities through themes like history, food, and literature. Imagine wandering through the historic streets of Dublin, where a knowledgeable local guide brings to life the stories of James Joyce and the city's literary heritage, or exploring the culinary delights of Cork, where each stop introduces you to traditional Irish fare and modern culinary innovations. These guided tours not only enrich your understanding of the places you visit, but also provide a platform for engaging with stories and anecdotes that might otherwise remain hidden in the hustle of independent exploration. Similarly, in smaller towns such as Kilkenny or Galway, walking tours can help you uncover hidden gems and local favorites, from ancient ruins tucked away in side streets to family-run bakeries with the best scones you've ever tasted.

For those who prefer the freedom of exploring at their own pace, Ireland offers abundant resources for planning self-guided walks, both in urban settings and the rolling countryside. Comprehensive walking guides and detailed maps are available both online and locally at tourist offices, providing routes that highlight major landmarks as well as lesser-known attractions. Apps and websites dedicated to outdoor explorations in Ireland often feature user-rated trails, complete with difficulty ratings, points of interest, and even tips on where to find the best coffee along the route. Whether it's tracing the architectural beauty of Limerick's Georgian Quarter or meandering through the wild, scenic trails of the Beara Peninsula, self-guided walking routes allow you to craft an adventure that suits your interests and physical ability, giving you control over your day and the flexibility to stop and admire the view, ponder over a historic site, or simply relax in a picturesque spot whenever you choose.

Joining a local hiking club or group can enhance your walking experience significantly, especially if you're keen to explore more remote or challenging landscapes safely. These clubs often organize regular group walks, ranging from gentle strolls suitable for all fitness levels to more strenuous hikes through some of Ireland's most stunning and rugged terrain. Participating in these walks assures you of safety in numbers and offers the camaraderie of fellow hiking enthusiasts and the guidance of experienced locals who know the trails well. Many of these clubs welcome visitors, providing an excellent opportunity to meet new people and learn about the local area from those who know it best. Additionally, club walks often venture into areas less frequented by tourists, providing a more authentic experience of the Irish countryside and its natural beauty.

Ireland's walking festivals are another fantastic avenue for immersing yourself in the walking culture of the country, catering to a range of interests and abilities. These festivals, held annually in various counties, celebrate walking and the outdoors with a series of guided walks and related events. For instance, the Mourne International Walking Festival in County Down offers routes that cater to all levels, from scenic paths suitable for families to challenging mountain treks, all led by knowledgeable guides who enhance the experience with their local insight and expertise. These festivals not only provide structured walking experiences in some of Ireland's most picturesque settings but also include social events, such as talks, music sessions, and communal meals, making them a celebratory and social occasion as much as a physical activity. Whether you're a seasoned hiker looking to tackle new trails or a casual walker interested in enjoying the outdoors while learning about the local culture, Ireland's walking festivals offer a welcoming and enriching environment to explore the landscape on foot.

Island Hopping: A Guide to Ireland's Offshore Gems

Exploring Ireland's islands offers a unique perspective on the country's diverse landscapes and rich cultural tapestry. Each island has its own character and history, providing a distinct experience far removed from the mainland's hustle. To begin your island-hopping adventure, understanding the ferry services that connect these gems to the mainland is essential. Operators like Aran Island Ferries and Rathlin Island Ferry provide regular services, with schedules that vary seasonally—more frequent in summer and reduced in winter. Booking in advance, especially during peak tourist seasons, is highly recommended to secure your spot. It's also wise to check the weather forecasts, as services can be disrupted by poor weather conditions. For those planning to visit multiple islands, consider purchasing a hop-on, hop-off pass where available, which offers flexibility and savings for extensive explorations.

The islands off the coast of Ireland are treasure troves of natural beauty and ancient culture. The Aran Islands, with their stark landscapes and strong Gaelic traditions, are a highlight. Here, Inis Mór, the largest island, offers attractions like Dún Aonghasa, a prehistoric fort perched dramatically on a cliff edge, providing stunning ocean views. The smaller Inis Meáin and Inis Oírr boast a more intimate experience of island life, with fewer tourists and abundant peaceful spots. Farther south, Skellig Michael, a UNESCO World Heritage Site, captivates visitors with its well-preserved monastic ruins and the surrounding waters teeming with birdlife. Rathlin Island, off the coast of County Antrim in Northern Ireland, offers a quieter escape, with its inviting walking trails and the famed West Light Seabird Centre, where puffins, guillemots, and razorbills can be observed in their natural habitat.

Planning your visit to these islands requires careful consideration, especially regarding what to pack. Weather on the islands can be even more unpredictable than on the mainland, with sudden changes that can catch the unprepared visitor off guard. Essential items include waterproof clothing and sturdy footwear, as well as layers that can be easily added or removed. Given the limited shopping resources on the islands, it's crucial to bring all necessary medications, and a first aid kit, and to stock up on any specific dietary items before departure. Bringing cash is also a good idea since ATM facilities can be rare, and not all places may accept credit cards. For those interested in birdwatching or wildlife photography, binoculars and a good camera with a zoom lens are must-haves to fully appreciate the rich biodiversity these islands offer.

When it comes to accommodations, Ireland's islands provide a range of options, from cozy, traditional cottages to modern eco-lodges. These island stays offer more than just a place to sleep—

they are part of the experience, imbued with the character and charm of their surroundings. On the Aran Islands, for example, staying in a traditional thatched cottage lets you live like a local, with stone walls and peat fires that speak of the islands' heritage. For those looking for a more luxurious experience, the eco-lodges on islands like Inis Meáin offer sustainable yet comfortable alternatives, with stunning views and eco-friendly practices that ensure your stay is both indulgent and conscientious. Booking these unique accommodations in advance is highly recommended, particularly during peak months, to avoid disappointment and to secure a spot at some of the more exclusive properties. As you settle into these accommodations, the slower pace of island life becomes a palpable rhythm, inviting you to disconnect from the rush of everyday life and reconnect with nature and tranquility.

Exploring the islands off Ireland's coast offers a journey through breathtaking landscapes, ancient histories, and vibrant wildlife, each island with its own story to tell. From the logistical ease provided by efficient ferry services to the immersive experiences of unique local accommodations, island hopping in Ireland is an adventure that promises both relaxation and discovery. With each island offering its own array of sights, sounds, and stories, your travels will be filled with moments of awe and appreciation, deepening your connection to the natural beauty and rich cultural heritage that Ireland proudly preserves.

Using Tech to Navigate: Apps and Online Resources

In today's digital age, exploring Ireland is made significantly more accessible and enriching with the aid of technology designed to enhance your travel experience. A suite of sophisticated apps and online resources can transform your smartphone or tablet into a virtual tour guide, navigator, and cultural encyclopedia, all at your fingertips. For instance, real-time public transport apps such as Transport for Ireland's Real Time Ireland app provide up-to-the-minute updates on bus and train schedules, helping you plan your journeys efficiently and avoid unnecessary delays. These apps often include detailed route maps and estimated arrival times, ensuring that you can move seamlessly from one destination to the next with confidence.

Moreover, for those moments when public transport isn't an option, apps like Free Now and Uber offer reliable taxi services across Ireland's major cities. With just a few taps, you can book a ride and track its arrival in real-time, providing a convenient and safe mode of transport, especially during the late hours or when you are laden with shopping bags from visiting local markets. Additionally, for the environmentally conscious traveler or those simply looking to add a bit of physical activity to their day, bike-sharing programs such as Dublin Bikes or Cork's Coke Zero Bikes can be accessed through respective apps that show the location of bike stations and the availability of bikes in real time, making cycling around the cities both enjoyable and hassle-free.

Navigating without an internet connection can be a challenge, especially in more remote areas of Ireland where mobile coverage might be spotty. Offline map apps such as Google Maps or Maps.me become invaluable in such situations, allowing you to download comprehensive maps that can be accessed without needing to connect to the internet. These apps not only provide directions but also highlight points of interest, from historic sites and parks to restaurants and cafes, ensuring that you can explore with the assurance that you won't miss out on anything note-worthy due to a lack of data access.

Cultural exploration in Ireland is enriched by apps that delve into the country's rich history and vibrant cultural scene. Apps like Rick Steves' Audio Europe offer narrated walking tours of major Irish cities, providing context and background that bring historic sites to life. For language enthusiasts or those keen to connect more deeply with the local population, apps like Duolingo or Memrise offer introductory lessons in the Irish language, enabling you to learn basic greetings and phrases that can open doors to warmer interactions with locals. Furthermore, for those eager to immerse themselves in Ireland's literary heritage, the JoyceWays app offers a guided literary tour of Dublin, tracing the steps of James Joyce's characters in "Ulysses" and providing insights into the author's connection to the city.

An integral part of the Irish experience is participating in the myriad events and festivals that showcase the country's rich traditions and contemporary creativity. Event finder apps and websites like Eventbrite or Meetup can be especially useful for keeping track of happenings around town, from music festivals and art exhibitions to local food fairs and historical reenactments. These platforms not only allow you to browse events by date and interest but also offer the convenience of online bookings, ensuring that you have all the details and tickets sorted well in advance of your visit.

As this chapter on using technology to navigate Ireland concludes, it's clear that integrating these digital tools into your travel plans can dramatically enhance your experience. From real-time transport updates and offline maps to cultural guides and event finders, each app and resource offers a unique function that, when combined, provides a comprehensive and accessible way to explore Ireland. With these digital companions at your disposal, you are well-equipped to discover the beauty, history, and culture of Ireland in a way that is both deep and broad, ensuring that every aspect of your journey is enriched and your travels are smooth and memorable. As we transition from the digital exploration of Ireland to the next chapter, where we will dive into the enchanting world of Irish festivals and events, the journey continues to unfold, promising new adventures and insights at every turn.

CHAPTER 6

ACCOMMODATIONS UNVEILED: FROM CASTLES TO COTTAGES

Imagine waking to the sound of morning dew dripping off ancient stone walls and the distant echo of falcon calls as they soar across wide, majestic landscapes. Staying in a castle in Ireland isn't just about luxurious accommodations; it's about stepping back in time, enveloping yourself in history, and living like royalty, if only for a night. This chapter will guide you through the grandiose world of castle stays, from the opulent halls echoing with tales of yesteryear to the hidden whispers of corridors that have witnessed centuries pass by. Here, every stone and tapestry tells a story, inviting you to become part of its legacy.

Castle Stays: Living Like Irish Royalty

Historic Castle Hotels

The concept of staying in a castle hotel transports you to a time of lords and ladies, grand banquets, and secret trysts. Ireland's countryside is dotted with these historic fortresses that have been transformed into luxurious hotels, each offering guests a unique glimpse into the past coupled with the amenities of modern-day luxury. Imagine sleeping in a four-poster bed under tapestried ceilings, wandering through manicured gardens that have entertained nobility for centuries, and dining in opulent halls where knights once feasted. Castle hotels like Ashford Castle in County Mayo and Dromoland Castle in County Clare are not just places to stay; they are destinations that offer a deeper connection to Irish heritage and culture, beautifully preserved and thoughtfully integrated into the luxury experience.

Booking Tips

Securing a stay in one of these majestic accommodations requires some planning. The best times to visit often depend on what you're seeking from your experience. For solitude and potentially lower rates, consider booking during the off-peak seasons, such as early spring or late autumn. The summer months, while offering robust services and lush landscapes, also bring higher demand and rates. Booking early is crucial, especially if you aim to participate in special events like medieval banquets or Christmas feasts, which are immensely popular and often sell out months in advance. Many castles also host unique events like historical reenactments or themed weekends, providing an even richer experience, so aligning your booking with these events can enhance your stay significantly.

Unique Features

The allure of castle stays goes beyond just luxurious accommodations; it's also about the unique features and activities that you can partake in. Many castle hotels offer experiences that transport you back in time, such as falconry, the sport of kings, where you can learn to handle majestic birds of prey under the guidance of expert falconers. Others might offer archery lessons on the castle grounds or horseback riding through sprawling estates. Inside, guided historical tours can help you uncover the rich past of these storied walls, from secret passageways to tales of intrigue and rebellion. These activities enrich your stay and provide a deeper appreciation of the castle's historical significance, making your visit a truly immersive journey into the past.

Budget Options

Experiencing the grandeur of castle living doesn't always have to come with a royal price tag. For those traveling on a budget, consider staying in lesser-known castles that offer a similar historical ambiance at a fraction of the cost. Another option is to look for last-minute deals or off-season discounts, when prices can be significantly lower. Some castles offer "castle-hostel" hybrids, where you can enjoy the castle environment in more modest, shared accommodations. Additionally, staying for more than one night often unlocks discounted rates, and packages that include meals or activities can also provide value while enhancing your experience. By exploring these options, you can indulge in the luxury of a castle stay while adhering to your budget, making your royal dreams a feasible and memorable part of your Irish adventure.

As you explore the possibilities of castle stays in Ireland, imagine yourself sipping a hot beverage by a giant hearth, the walls around you steeped in history and the luxuries of today within arm's reach. This unique blend of past and present is not just about seeing a castle but experiencing it as those who once lived there might have, albeit with the added comforts of modern amenities. Whether you're seeking a romantic getaway, a touch of adventure, or a peaceful retreat, castle accommodations provide a gateway to a different era, offering a stay that is as enriching as it is luxurious, set against some of the most beautiful backdrops Ireland has to offer.

Cozy Cottages: A Home Away From Home

In the heart of Ireland's verdant landscapes and amongst its whispering shores, a different kind of accommodation beckons those who seek intimacy with the land and a quiet nook to call their own. Cottage rentals in Ireland offer a charming and deeply personal way to experience the country's natural beauty and cultural warmth. Each cottage tells a story, crafted from the stones and woods of its locale, and invites you into a living space that feels like your own Irish home. Whether nestled in a secluded corner of a wildflower meadow or perched quaintly in a serene seaside village, cottages offer privacy, comfort, and an immersive atmosphere that larger hotels simply can't replicate. Here, the day starts with the gentle lull of the local birds and ends with a cup of tea by a crackling fireplace, the day's adventures turning into evening reflections.

Cottages in Ireland are postcards of the picturesque, offering not just a place to stay but a canvas on which to paint your memories. Imagine a quaint cottage by the rugged cliffs of Moher, where the Atlantic's roar lulls you to sleep, or a rustic hideaway in the rolling hills of Connemara, where the mountains meet the sky in a spectacle of nature's artistry. For those drawn to the charm of the Irish countryside, cottages in counties like Kerry and Cork provide gateways to exploring the scenic Ring of Kerry or the tranquil beauty of the Beara Peninsula. Not to be outdone, the East Coast offers gems like the thatched cottages in Wexford, where history and modernity blend seamlessly, providing easy access to ancient castles and vibrant local markets. Each location promises a unique backdrop to your stay, ensuring that your accommodation is not just a place to rest but a significant part of your Irish adventure.

When you step into an Irish cottage, you step into a fully equipped home that marries traditional aesthetics with modern amenities. Typical features might include cozy living spaces with wood-burning stoves, sun-drenched conservatories where you can enjoy a morning coffee, and charming kitchens equipped with everything you need for a night in. Many cottages also offer private gardens, perfect for those long summer evenings spent outdoors or simply for a moment of solitude with a good book. It's common for hosts to provide a welcome basket filled with local treats like freshly baked soda bread, farm eggs, and homemade jams, making your arrival not just comfortable but delightful. For those who enjoy cooking, the self-catering aspect allows you to try your hand at local recipes with ingredients sourced from nearby markets, turning meals into an exploration of Irish culinary traditions.

Finding the perfect cottage requires navigating a variety of booking platforms that cater to different needs and preferences. Websites like Airbnb and Vrbo are popular for their wide range of listings and user reviews, offering insights into what you can expect from your stay. For those seeking cottages that are vetted for quality and charm, specialized agencies like Imagine Ireland and Irish Cottage Holidays provide selections that are not only beautiful but come with detailed descriptions and customer support that can assist in making your stay perfect. Direct booking through a cottage's own website can sometimes offer the best rates and the opportunity for a more personal interaction with the host, often leading to valuable local tips and recommendations. When booking, consider your needs regarding space, location, and amenities, and always communicate directly with the host to clarify any details. This ensures that when you arrive, the cottage meets all your expectations, allowing you to settle in and start enjoying your Irish retreat right away.

As you weave through the options and consider the landscapes that call to you, remember that each cottage, with its unique features and settings, offers more than just a place to stay. It offers a chance to live like a local, to weave yourself into the fabric of rural Ireland, and to create a retreat that feels like your own. In these cottages, the Ireland you explore by day becomes the Ireland you live in by night, each moment at your own pace, each experience deeply personal. Whether it's waking up to the sound of the sea or watching the sunset over the mountains, your cottage becomes a home in the heart of Ireland, enveloping you in its warmth and beauty.

Budget Beauties: Affordable Hostels and B&Bs

In the heart of Ireland's vibrant towns and serene landscapes, hostels and bed and breakfasts (B&Bs) offer not just a place to stay but a doorway to genuine Irish hospitality. These accommodations are perfect for travelers who wish to immerse themselves in local culture without stretching their budget. Hostels, in particular, are a fantastic option for those seeking a social atmosphere where stories and tips are exchanged freely among travelers from all corners of the world. Imagine the camaraderie of cooking meals together in a communal kitchen or planning spontaneous adventures based on recommendations from new friends. Many hostels also offer organized events like pub crawls or city tours, enhancing the social experience and providing opportunities to explore the locale in a group setting. The modern Irish hostel often includes amenities like free Wi-Fi, secure lockers, and comfortable common areas, making them suitable for a range of travelers from solo adventurers to groups.

Bed and breakfasts, on the other hand, offer a more intimate setting, often run by locals who provide personalized insights into the area's attractions and history. Each morning, you can savor a hearty Irish breakfast prepared from locally sourced ingredients—a true taste of traditional Irish cooking. B&Bs frequently embody the character of their locales, whether it's a Victorian townhouse with period features or a countryside home with stunning views of the rolling hills. The charm of B&Bs lies in their warm, personal service and the chance to experience Irish hospitality firsthand, making them a favored choice for those who seek a deeper connection to the places they visit.

When looking for top-rated hostels and B&Bs, consider establishments like the Galway City Hostel, positioned right next to the train station, making it incredibly convenient for explorers. It's known for its welcoming atmosphere and well-informed staff who are always ready to help with travel plans. In Dublin, the Generator Hostel stands out for its chic design and vibrant social events, which make it a hit among younger travelers. For a quieter, more scenic experience, the Sleepzone Hostel near Connemara offers access to some of Ireland's most beautiful landscapes. Among B&Bs, the Kilcoe Cottage in West Cork offers a picturesque retreat with stunning ocean views and homemade breakfasts that feature the best of local produce. In the bustling heart of Dublin, Ariel House stands as a Victorian-era jewel, offering elegant rooms and award-winning breakfasts, just a short stroll from the city's main attractions.

Securing the best rates for hostels and B&Bs in Ireland requires a few savvy strategies. Booking directly through a hostel or B&B's own website can often secure the best deals, as it saves the establishment from paying third-party fees, and they sometimes pass these savings on to their guests. Traveling during the shoulder seasons—spring and autumn—can also result in lower rates, plus you'll enjoy Ireland's natural beauty with fewer crowds. For those planning longer stays, many B&Bs and hostels offer discounts for extended bookings, so it's worth inquiring about these when you reserve. Additionally, always check for last-minute deals, as these can offer substantial savings, especially if you're flexible with your travel dates.

Understanding and respecting the etiquette of staying in shared accommodations ensures a pleasant experience for all. In hostels, be mindful of noise levels, especially late at night, and keep communal areas clean. Participating in hostel events or outings can greatly enhance your stay, helping you to make connections and discover local spots you might otherwise miss. In B&Bs, engaging with your hosts can enrich your understanding of the area, and many hosts appreciate when guests share their own stories and cultures. Simple acts like stripping the bed on your departure and thanking your hosts personally can leave a lasting good impression, fostering a sense of community and respect that is central to the ethos of B&B hospitality.

As you delve into the world of hostels and B&Bs across Ireland, each stay brings you closer to the heart of Irish culture, offering comfortable, budget-friendly accommodations that do not compromise on warmth or character. Whether you find yourself in a lively city hostel or a quaint countryside B&B, these experiences are bound to be among the highlights of your Irish adventure, filled with memorable encounters and the irreplaceable warmth of Irish hospitality.

Eco-Friendly Escapes: Sustainable Stays in Ireland

In an era where sustainability is not just appreciated but essential, Ireland offers an array of eco-friendly accommodations that allow you to enjoy its natural beauty responsibly. These green havens range from state-of-the-art eco-lodges nestled in expansive national parks to hotels in the heart of bustling cities that boast impressive green certifications. Staying at these places, you contribute to the preservation of the very landscapes and communities that make Ireland so enchanting. Properties like the Clifden Eco Beach Camping & Caravanning Park set the standard with their minimal environmental impact, utilizing wind and solar power to reduce reliance on non-renewable energy sources. Similarly, the BrookLodge & Macreddin Village in County Wicklow not only offers luxury in the lap of nature but does so with a commitment to sustainability, featuring organic restaurants and eco-spa treatments that use natural local ingredients.

As you explore these green accommodations, it's crucial to look for sustainable practices that align with your environmental values. Renewable energy use is a key factor; many eco-friendly properties in Ireland harness the power of solar, wind, or even geothermal energy to heat buildings and water, reducing their carbon footprint. Water conservation is another practice to consider; facilities that employ rainwater harvesting systems or low-flow fixtures help preserve Ireland's precious water resources. Additionally, waste reduction efforts such as comprehensive recycling programs and initiatives to minimize food waste can significantly influence the sustainability of an accommodation. When considering a place to stay, take the time to inquire about its sustainability practices, not only to ensure they match your expectations but also to encourage businesses to maintain and improve their environmental efforts.

For those keen to engage directly with Ireland's natural and cultural heritage in an environmentally conscious manner, look for properties that offer eco-friendly activities. Many eco-lodges and green hotels are not just places to stay but gateways to exploring the surrounding environment without harming it. Activities might include guided nature walks that educate guests on local flora and fauna, birdwatching tours that highlight conservation efforts, or even hands-on experiences like organic farming workshops where you can learn about sustainable agriculture practices. The Burren Perfumery, located near many eco-friendly cottages, offers workshops on making perfumes and lotions using local organic herbs, providing a unique insight into sustainable production practices. Engaging in these activities not only enriches your travel experience but also supports local economies and conservation efforts, making your stay beneficial to both you and the host community.

Booking an eco-friendly stay in Ireland requires a bit of research and thoughtful consideration. Start by identifying what sustainability means to you and what practices are most important for your comfort and ethical peace of mind. Online platforms dedicated to eco-tourism, such as Ecobnb or Green Pearls, can be invaluable resources, offering a curated list of verified sustainable accommodations. These platforms often provide detailed information about the environmental initiatives of each property, making it easier to find a place that meets your criteria. When contacting a property, don't hesitate to ask about their sustainability certifications, such as the EU Ecolabel or Green Hospitality Award, which can provide reassurance of their commitment to environmental standards. Additionally, consider reading reviews from previous guests, focusing on their mentions of how the property's eco-friendly practices affected their stay. This firsthand insight can be instrumental in deciding where to book, ensuring that your eco-friendly escape is as rewarding as it is responsible, allowing you to enjoy Ireland's natural beauty while preserving it for future generations.

Family-Friendly Lodgings: Keeping Everyone Happy

Traveling with family, especially children, turns an ordinary journey into a treasure trove of memories and shared experiences. Understanding the distinct needs of families, many accommodations across Ireland have tailored their environments to enhance comfort and convenience for all ages. Family-friendly hotels and resorts often feature a variety of amenities designed specifically to keep children engaged and parents relaxed. Picture expansive grounds equipped with playgrounds where children can expend their energy and interact with peers under the safe watch of experienced staff. Swimming pools with child-safe features provide a perfect setting for family fun, ensuring that the little ones are entertained under controlled and secure conditions. Moreover, family rooms in these accommodations are thoughtfully designed to offer ample space and often include convenient facilities such as cribs, high chairs, and even kid-friendly bath products, ensuring that families feel at home.

When selecting a place to stay, the location of your accommodation plays a crucial role in how you experience Ireland with your family. Staying in a locale that is central or has easy access to major attractions can significantly reduce travel time and stress. Consider accommodations that are within walking distance or a short public transport ride away from family-friendly attractions such as zoos, parks, and interactive museums. This proximity allows for flexible planning, where you can easily return to your lodging for midday breaks or unexpected needs, making the trip more enjoyable and manageable. Additionally, accommodations near public transport routes enhance your ability to explore further afield, visiting historical sites and natural landscapes that offer educational and fun experiences for children and adults alike.

Securing family-friendly accommodations often comes with opportunities to avail of special deals and discounts, which can make a significant difference in budgeting for your trip. Many hotels and resorts offer family packages that include accommodations, meals, and sometimes even tickets to nearby attractions at a reduced rate. Look for deals where children stay for free or at a discounted rate when sharing a room with parents, which is common in many family-oriented hotels. Booking outside of peak tourist seasons can also yield more favorable rates and packages, with the added benefit of experiencing Ireland's attractions without the crowds. Always inquire directly with the accommodation for any ongoing promotions or possible upgrades available at check-in, as this can often lead to better deals and enhanced experiences during your stay.

Dining with children can sometimes be a challenge, but many family-friendly accommodations in Ireland go to great lengths to ensure a pleasant dining experience for all ages. Restaurants within these properties often feature children's menus that offer a variety of healthy, kid-approved options, ensuring that even the pickiest eaters have choices they will enjoy. Flexible dining hours cater to families who may not adhere to conventional meal times, especially with younger children. Additionally, the welcoming atmosphere in these dining settings often means that other families are present, creating a relaxed environment where children's laughter is part of the mealtime charm, and parents can feel at ease knowing their children are welcome. This focus on accommodating families extends beyond the menu, with staff trained to interact positively with young guests, making dining out a stress-free and enjoyable part of your travel.

In every aspect, from the thoughtful amenities and strategic locations to special deals and accommodating dining experiences, family-friendly lodgings in Ireland offer more than just a place to stay. They provide a supportive base from which families can explore, relax, and create lasting memories together in the heart of one of the most beautiful countries in the world. Whether it's returning to a cozy room after a day of adventure or enjoying a family meal in a welcoming restaurant, these accommodations understand and cater to the unique dynamics of traveling with children, ensuring that every family leaves with a deeper bond and joyful stories to tell.

Unique Irish Experiences: Lighthouses to Monasteries

Ireland, a land woven with tales of the sea and sanctity, offers some of the most unique accommodations that go beyond the ordinary, inviting you to not just visit, but to immerse yourself in its distinct narrative. Consider the experience of staying in a lighthouse. Perched on rugged cliffs, these beacons have guided sailors through tumultuous waters for centuries and now invite travelers to experience life at the edge of the world. Places like the Wicklow Head Lighthouse allow you to literally live in a lighthouse keeper's quarters, transformed into cozy, modern accommodations. Here, the panoramic views of the relentless Atlantic Ocean and the serene solitude make for a reflective retreat, where the rhythmic sweep of the lighthouse beam at night ensures a connection with maritime history that is as profound as it is picturesque.

Monastic retreats offer another pathway to peace, this time through the spiritual tranquility and simplicity that can only be found within the ancient walls of Ireland's historic monasteries. These retreats, such as the one offered by the Glenstal Abbey in County Limerick, provide a chance to step away from the clamor of modern life and engage with a lifestyle that has been practiced for centuries. Guests are invited to join in the daily rhythms of monastic life, which may include participation in prayer sessions, silent meditation, and walks through sacred grounds. The spartan yet serene accommodations encourage introspection and connection, offering a stark contrast to the often hectic pace of contemporary travel and an opportunity to reconnect with oneself in profound silence and historic surroundings.

In recent years, the trend of glamping and eco pods has captured the imagination of those who wish to combine the rustic appeal of camping with the comforts of modern amenities. Throughout Ireland, this style of accommodation has flourished, offering luxurious tents, yurts, and eco pods that provide a blissful balance of comfort and immersion in nature. The Eco Pod at Top of the Rock Pod Páirc in West Cork exemplifies this trend, where you can stay in a custom-designed pod that blends into the landscape, offering stunning views of the surrounding countryside. These eco-friendly pods are equipped with the essentials, including heating and comfortable bedding, ensuring a cozy stay regardless of the weather, all while keeping environmental impact to a minimum.

For those seeking truly unconventional stays, Ireland does not disappoint. The country's rich history and vibrant culture have transformed various structures into unique accommodations. Imagine spending the night in a converted Victorian railway carriage at the Old Railway Station in County Donegal, where the charm of a bygone era is preserved in meticulously restored interiors. Alternatively, treehouses and converted barns, such as the luxurious Treehouse at Castlecomer Discovery Park or the rustic charm of the Barn at Le Cheile in County Mayo, provide a whimsical escape into settings that are as enchanting as they are unusual. These accommodations not only offer a place to stay but encapsulate stories and lifestyles that enhance your travel experience, making your Irish adventure truly memorable.

As you explore these unique accommodations, each stay becomes a chapter in your own Irish tale, rich with the beauty of rugged coastlines, the echoes of ancient chants, and the soft rustle of leaves in a countryside retreat. Whether it's the solitude of a lighthouse, the spiritual sanctuary of a monastery, the chic comfort of a glamping pod, or the quirky charm of a converted barn, these experiences invite you to engage with Ireland in ways that go beyond the conventional, offering perspectives that are as varied and enriching as the landscape itself.

As this chapter on unique Irish accommodations draws to a close, we reflect on the myriad ways in which staying in places like lighthouses, monasteries, eco pods, and other unconventional lodgings can deepen your connection not only to the landscapes of Ireland but also to its cultural heritage and historical depth. These accommodations are not just about a place to sleep—they are gateways to the soul of Ireland, offering insights and experiences that resonate long after you leave. As you turn the pages of this guide and continue your exploration of Ireland, remember that each choice in accommodation can enrich your journey, adding layers of understanding and enjoyment to your adventure in the Emerald Isle.

CHAPTER 7

FROM FARM TO TABLE: IRELAND'S CULINARY REVOLUTION

Imagine standing in the lush, green heartland of Ireland, where the air is fragrant with the earthy scent of pasture and the rich aroma of a nearby cheese maker's workshop. Here, the Irish culinary landscape is painted with broad strokes of tradition and innovation, creating a vibrant tableau that invites you to delve deeper into its flavors and stories. This chapter explores the exquisite world of Irish cheeses, guiding you through pastures where cows roam freely, and artisanal cheese makers craft their magic. It's a journey that promises not just taste experiences but a profound connection to the land and its people.

The Best of Irish Cheeses: A Tasting Tour

Artisanal Variety

Ireland's cheese-making heritage is as rich and varied as the land-scapes from which it springs. From the soft, tangy young cheeses to the hard, aged varieties, Irish cheeses encompass a palette of flavors that reflect the regional diversities and cheese-making traditions that have evolved over centuries. Renowned cheese makers like Gubbeen and Cashel Blue are just the tip of the iceberg. Each region boasts its own specialties, with local artisans pushing the boundaries of taste and texture. The Durrus Cheese, made in West Cork, offers a creamy, complex flavor developed in the unique microclimate of the Sheepshead Peninsula. In contrast, the rugged landscapes of County Tipperary produce the robust, award-winning Cooleeney cheese. This cheese serves as a perfect embodiment of the local terroir, capturing the essence of its origin.

Tasting Locations

To truly savor these cheeses, one must venture into the heart of Ireland's cheese country—visiting farms, attending tastings, and exploring the local markets where these artisanal products take center stage. The English Market in Cork City, a venerable institution since 1788, provides not only a feast for the senses but also a chance to meet the producers who are the lifeblood of Ireland's cheese scene. Here, at stalls like the Farmgate Café, you can indulge in a carefully curated cheese board accompanied by a glass of local wine. For a more hands-on experience, a visit to the Little Milk Company in County Waterford offers insights into the cooperative efforts of organic dairy farmers across Ireland, with tastings that highlight the distinctive qualities of their produce.

Pairing Suggestions

Pairing these cheeses with the right accompaniment can elevate your tasting experience to new heights. A robust Cashel Blue sings when paired with a sweet and tart apple chutney, while the creamy textures of a young Gubbeen are beautifully complemented by a crisp Irish craft cider. Local sommeliers and chefs often recommend pairing Ballylisk Triple Cream with a glass of chilled Irish pear cider, creating a balance of flavors that enhances the characteristics of both the cheese and the cider. For those who prefer wine, a glass of aromatic Irish mead can bring out the subtler notes of a mature Cáis na Tíre sheep's cheese.

Cheese-Making Workshops

For those inspired not just to taste but to create, Ireland offers a myriad of cheese-making workshops that invite you to roll up your sleeves and learn the craft firsthand. These workshops, often hosted by the very artisans who supply Ireland's finest restaurants and shops, provide an immersive experience into the world of cheese making. At the Ballymaloe Cookery School in County Cork, you can spend a day learning the delicate art of curdling, pressing, and aging under the guidance of expert cheese makers. Not only do these workshops offer a deeper appreciation of the craft, but they also allow you to take a piece of Ireland's culinary heritage home with you, in the form of your very own handmade cheese.

As you explore the rich tapestry of Ireland's cheese culture, from the lush, green fields of the countryside to the bustling markets of its cities, you embark on a culinary journey that offers both depth and breadth in understanding and appreciation. This chapter, a tribute to the art and craft of Irish cheese making, invites you to indulge in the flavors, stories, and traditions that make Ireland a true haven for cheese lovers.

Ireland's Craft Beer and Distilleries: Beyond Guinness

In recent years, Ireland has witnessed a dynamic revolution not just in its landscapes and technology, but profoundly in its breweries and distilleries, reshaping an age-old drinking culture known worldwide primarily for Guinness. This new wave, known as the Craft Beer Renaissance, sees local brewers crafting beers that are as rich in variety as they are in flavor. Across the green expanses of Ireland, from the rugged coasts of Donegal to the historic streets of Dublin, small breweries like The White Hag in Sligo and Galway Bay Brewery are crafting unique blends that push the boundaries of traditional beer. These establishments are experimenting with local ingredients, from Irish barley to locally harvested seaweed, creating beers that are not just a drink but a storytelling medium about the land itself. For any enthusiast eager to explore this scene, a visit to the Franciscan Well Brewpub in Cork offers an extensive selection of craft beers coupled with a deep dive into the brewing process through guided tours and tasting sessions. Here, you can savor the award-winning Rebel Red Ale and learn about the nuances that give this brew its distinctive taste.

As the craft beer scene burgeons, so too does the distillery boom in Ireland, marking a renaissance for spirits like whiskey, gin, and beyond. New distilleries are opening their doors, where the air is thick with the aroma of fermenting grains and botanicals, signaling the rich, spirited concoctions being birthed. The Dingle Distillery in County Kerry stands out for its artisanal approach, offering gins and vodkas that are as unique to the palate as the landscape is to the eye. Their tours provide an insight into the meticulous craft of distillation, followed by tastings that highlight the subtle notes of locally sourced botanicals. For whiskey lovers, a trip to the Teeling Distillery in the heart of Dublin offers a modern take on an ancient craft, with their innovative whiskey aging processes that involve various types of casks, including those previously used for wine, rum, and even tequila, imparting complex flavors that challenge and delight the connoisseur's palate.

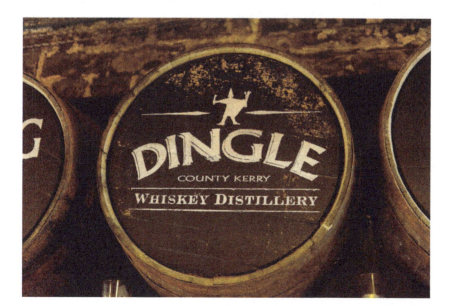

The heart of Ireland's craft beverage culture often beats strongest in its pubs, where the fusion of history, music, and local brews creates an atmosphere that is both intoxicating and welcoming. Pubs like The Cobblestone in Dublin are not just places to drink, but cultural hubs where live traditional music provides the soundtrack to an evening of local craft beer and spirited conversations. Here, the taps flow with an array of local brews, each with a story, a favorite being the smooth and malty O'Hara's Irish Stout, perfect for a night of music and camaraderie. Another must-visit is Dick Mack's in Dingle, a pub that doubles as a leather shop by day and a lively bar by night, where you can enjoy a local gin while surrounded by the rich aroma of leather and the lively chatter of locals and tourists alike.

For those looking to fully immerse themselves in Ireland's craft beverage scene, the calendar is dotted with festivals that celebrate the country's brewing and distilling prowess. The Irish Craft Beer Festival, held annually in Dublin, is perhaps the largest gathering of craft brewers in Ireland, offering a chance to taste over 200 different beers, stouts, and ciders from all across the country. For spirit enthusiasts, the Galway Gin Festival showcases the finest gins from around Ireland, complete with masterclasses and tastings set against the backdrop of Galway's vibrant cultural scene. These festivals provide a platform for tasting, learning, and meeting the artisans behind the brews, each passionate about their craft and eager to share their knowledge and stories with you. As you traverse from one stall to another, from a hop-infused ale to a botanical-rich gin, each sip invites you deeper into the heart and soul of Ireland's craft beverage culture, a journey through flavors crafted by the land and its people.

Seafood Splendors: Ireland's Coastal Delights

Ireland's coastal regions, a spectacular canvas of crashing waves and rugged cliffs, serve as the backdrop to a dynamic seafood scene that is as integral to Irish cuisine as the grass-fed lamb and artisan cheeses. The cold, clean waters of the Atlantic are teeming with an array of seafood, offering a freshness and quality that is hard to surpass. From the world-renowned Galway oysters to the succulent Atlantic salmon, the variety of seafood available here reflects the natural bounty of Ireland's waters. Each bite of seafood carries the taste of the ocean and tells the story of the local communities whose lives and traditions are deeply intertwined with fishing.

For those eager to indulge in these marine delicacies, the culinary landscape of Ireland's coast is dotted with restaurants where the ocean's harvest is transformed into gastronomic masterpieces. In the quaint village of Howth, just outside Dublin, you can enjoy a meal at The Oar House, a favorite among locals and visitors alike. Here, the catch of the day might include tender crab claws, mussels steamed in white wine, or a hearty seafood chowder, each dish crafted to highlight the natural flavors of the sea. Further south, in Cork, the restaurant at Ballymaloe House offers a sophisticated menu featuring locally sourced seafood, such as Ballycotton fish that moves from sea to plate within hours. The experience of dining here is enhanced by the panoramic views of rolling fields and the distant sea, reminding you of the close connection between the land and the waters that provide these culinary treasures.

As you explore the Irish coast, a visit to one of the local seafood markets offers a glimpse into the vibrant culture of seafood consumption in Ireland. The English Market in Cork, with its bustling stalls adorned with ice-filled counters brimming with fish, shellfish, and seaweed, provides not just a place to buy fresh seafood but also a chance to learn about the different species and their culinary uses. Fishmongers, often from families who have been in the trade for generations, are masters of their craft and are usually eager to share their knowledge about how to pick the best seafood and offer tips on how to prepare it. At markets like these, you can find everything from hake to herrings, scallops to sole, each promising an adventure in cooking and eating.

For a truly immersive experience, consider joining a fishing tour or a seafood foraging expedition. These tours allow you to see where your food comes from, and you also get to participate in the age-old traditions of fishing and foraging that are still alive in many coastal communities. In County Galway, guided tours take you on a boat to catch mackerel or to forage for mussels and clams at low tide. These experiences often end with cooking sessions, where you can learn how to prepare your catch according to local traditions, turning your day's work into a delicious meal. This hands-on approach deepens your appreciation of Irish seafood and connects you with the people and practices that make Ireland's culinary culture so rich and inviting.

As you meander through the coastal towns, indulge in the seafood offerings, and interact with the people who make Ireland a haven for seafood lovers, you are doing more than just eating; you are engaging in a storied practice that continues to shape the cultural and culinary contours of this island nation. Whether it's shucking oysters by the shore or savoring a seafood feast in a cozy village pub, the seafood splendors of Ireland promise a journey of taste, tradition, and discovery.

Traditional Dishes with a Twist: Modern Irish Cuisine

In the vibrant kitchens of Ireland, a quiet revolution simmers as innovative chefs weave a tapestry of flavors that are redefining Irish cuisine. These culinary artists are not just cooking; they are reimagining the very essence of traditional Irish dishes through modern techniques and a fusion of international flavors. Picture a Dublin restaurant where a young chef, trained in the world's top culinary schools, takes the humble Irish stew and transforms it by slow-cooking local grass-fed beef with artisanal craft beer, adding a layer of caramelized onions for a subtle sweetness that complements the robustness of the meat. This dish, once a simple staple of the Irish diet, is now a complex narrative of Ireland's agricultural richness and global culinary influences.

The redefinition of classic dishes extends beyond stews. Consider the traditional Irish soda bread, a beloved companion to many a meal across the country. In the hands of a pioneering chef in Cork, this bread takes on a new life when combined with seaweed harvested from the nearby coast, infusing it with a salty crispness that echoes the Atlantic breeze. Similarly, colcannon, known for its comforting blend of mashed potatoes and kale or cabbage, is elevated in a Galway eatery where it's served alongside seared scallops caught fresh from Galway Bay, the dish garnished with a drizzle of truffle oil to add a touch of luxury that transforms the entire eating experience.

The farm-to-table movement flourishes robustly in Ireland, with restaurants committed to showcasing locally sourced ingredients through seasonal menus that speak of the land's bounty. In these establishments, the connection between the farmer and the chef is palpable, each dish served as a testament to their collaborative effort to deliver freshness and quality. One standout restaurant in the heart of the Wicklow Mountains offers a menu that changes with the seasons, ensuring that each ingredient used is fresh and at its peak. Here, you might enjoy a spring salad of tender baby greens, edible flowers, and a light vinaigrette made with local honey, each bite a burst of the season's colors and flavors.

Culinary Awards

The innovation and excellence of Irish chefs have not gone unnoticed on the international stage. Irish restaurants and their visionary chefs have garnered accolades and recognition, marking Ireland as a premier destination for gastronomy. An example is a restaurant in Limerick, which was awarded a Michelin star for its daring reinterpretation of Irish classics using molecular gastronomy techniques. Here, the chef artfully combines science and culinary art to create dishes that are visually spectacular and a delight to the palate. The restaurant's signature dish, a deconstructed Irish lamb stew, features lamb that is sous-vide to perfection, accompanied by a potato foam and carrot gel, each element a familiar flavor presented in an entirely new form.

As you explore the modern Irish culinary landscape, each meal becomes more than just an act of eating; it is an experience, a discovery of Ireland's culinary past and its dynamic present. Through the hands of its chefs, Ireland's traditional dishes continue to evolve, telling new stories, inviting locals and travelers alike to the table for a taste of the old and the new. Whether it's in the bustling cities or the quiet countryside, the revolution in the kitchen continues, promising more delights, more surprises, and an unending celebration of Irish food.

Ireland's Farmers' Markets: A Feast for the Senses

Strolling through one of Ireland's vibrant farmers' markets is akin to walking through a colorful gallery where each stall is a masterpiece of hues, aromas, and flavors. These markets serve as a bustling hub where the community gathers to buy food and celebrate the very essence of Irish agrarian life and artisanship. Each visit offers a sensory delight, with stalls brimming with everything from fresh organic vegetables and handcrafted cheeses to artisan breads and homemade jams. As you wander through locales such as the bustling Temple Bar Food Market in Dublin or the quaint Skibbereen Farmers Market in Cork, you're not merely shopping; you're partaking in a tradition that celebrates the seasonal bounty of Ireland's fertile soil.

The rhythm of these markets changes with the seasons, each bringing its own specialties to the forefront. Spring welcomes a burst of fresh greens such as spinach and wild garlic, which are perfect for revitalizing salads or a fresh pesto. Summer offers an abundance of choices with stalls laden with ripe strawberries and cherries, alongside vibrant peas and beans. Autumn introduces the heartier flavors of pumpkins and squashes, beautifully complemented by the last of the plump tomatoes and crisp apples. Winter might seem quieter, but it is rich with the offerings of root vegetables and hearty leeks, perfect for warming soups and stews. These seasonal rhythms dictate the life of the market and inspire the menus of local homes and restaurants, encouraging a culinary creativity that is inherently tied to the time of year.

Engaging with the producers at these markets transforms a simple purchase into a rich exchange of knowledge and stories. Take the time to speak with someone like Tom, a third-generation apple grower whose family has tended orchards in County Armagh for over a century, or chat with Sarah, a young artisan who started her own business creating organic goat's cheese in County Galway. These interactions enrich your understanding of the food you buy, connecting you to the land and the people who work it with passion and pride. These farmers and artisans are the unsung heroes of Ireland's food scene, champions of sustainability and biodiversity, and custodians of heritage and craft. Their stories of challenges and triumphs add layers of depth and appreciation to every bite of their produce.

In the comfort of your self-catering accommodation, the ingredients purchased from these markets can transform into a delightful exploration of Irish cuisine. Imagine using freshly picked herbs and vibrant vegetables to craft a traditional Irish vegetable soup. Or perhaps, using artisanal bread to create a robust sandwich filled with local cheese and chutney, accompanied by a side of hand-picked salad greens. For those with a sweet tooth, the challenge of baking a traditional Irish apple cake with apples bought directly from the grower can be a rewarding endeavor. These culinary experiments enhance your stay and deepen your connection to Irish food culture, turning each meal into a celebration of local produce and artisanal craftsmanship.

Navigating through Ireland's farmers' markets is more than just an activity; it's an immersion into a world where food is revered and shared with joy, where every stall tells a story, and every flavor carries the essence of Ireland. As you weave through the crowds, sample the fresh produce, and meet the faces behind the food, you become part of a community that thrives on the connection to the land and to each other. This is where the true flavor of Ireland comes alive, not just in the food but in the spirit of the place and its people.

Cooking Classes: Bringing Irish Flavors Home

In the vibrant heart of Ireland, where culinary traditions meld seamlessly with innovative approaches, cooking classes offer a delightful avenue for both locals and visitors to immerse themselves in the epicurean culture. These classes range from brief, half-day introductions that cover the basics of traditional Irish cooking to comprehensive culinary courses that span several weeks, providing deep dives into advanced cooking techniques and regional specialties. Imagine spending a morning in a rustic kitchen in County Cork, where under the guidance of a local chef, you and your fellow culinary enthusiasts learn to craft the perfect Irish soda bread, its crust golden and satisfyingly crisp. Or perhaps, partaking in a more extended course in Dublin's top culinary school, where the secrets of modern Irish cuisine are unfolded through hands-on sessions and mentorship from master chefs.

The focus on regional specialties in many of these classes allows you to explore Ireland's culinary diversity. Each region offers its unique flavors and cooking methods, influenced by local history, geography, and available resources. In the coastal towns of the West, for instance, cooking classes might center around seafood, teaching you how to prepare dishes like seared scallops with a dulse seaweed butter, or traditional mackerel paté. In contrast, classes in the fertile midlands might focus on farm-to-table cooking, utilizing local meats and dairy along with fresh produce to create hearty, comforting dishes that speak of the land's bounty. These sessions not only teach cooking skills but also imbue a sense of place and tradition, enriching your understanding of the regional variations that color Ireland's culinary landscape.

For those looking to refine their culinary skills under the tutelage of renowned chefs, Ireland offers a range of professional workshops that cater to more experienced cooks seeking to elevate their technique. These workshops often take place in state-of-the-art facilities and are led by chefs who have earned accolades in Ireland and abroad. Participants might find themselves mastering the intricacies of molecular gastronomy, exploring the delicate art of pastry making, or perfecting the balance of flavors in complex dishes that could grace the tables of high-end restaurants. These sessions enhance your culinary skills and provide insights into the contemporary trends that influence modern Irish cooking, offering inspiration that transcends geographical boundaries.

Cooking classes in Ireland also provide wonderful opportunities for families or groups traveling together. Many culinary schools and independent chefs offer classes that are designed to be fun and engaging for participants of all ages. These family-friendly options often include simpler tasks that allow younger participants to get involved, such as decorating cupcakes or making simple, tasty snacks like fruit scones. These activities not only introduce children to the joys of cooking but also encourage teamwork and creativity, making for a memorable family experience. Moreover, cooking together in a relaxed, supportive environment allows families to bond, turning a recipe into a shared adventure that ends with the satisfaction of a meal enjoyed together.

As you explore the various cooking classes available across Ireland, you realize that these experiences offer much more than just culinary education. They are a gateway to understanding Ireland's rich culinary heritage and its dynamic present, providing a hands-on way to connect with the food, the people, and the culture. Whether you're kneading dough under the watchful eye of a seasoned baker or plating a dish that combines Irish ingredients with international techniques, these classes offer a taste of Ireland that is profound and personal. They invite you to bring a piece of Ireland into your kitchen, transforming the flavors and techniques learned into meals that can be recreated and savored, long after you've returned home.

In wrapping up this chapter on the transformative experiences offered by Ireland's culinary classes, we touch upon the essence of what makes these experiences so enriching. From the hands-on learning and discovery of local and regional specialties to the guidance provided by accomplished chefs and the joyous communal atmosphere of cooking with family and friends, each element contributes to a deeper appreciation of Ireland's culinary arts. As you carry these recipes and techniques home, they serve not only as souvenirs, but as lasting connections to the Irish culture and its generous spirit. Moving forward, the journey through Ireland's culinary landscape continues to unfold, promising further exploration of its rich flavors and storied traditions in the chapters to come.

CHAPTER 8

CELEBRATING IRISH
FESTIVALS AND EVENTS

As the first light of dawn creeps across the cobblestone streets of Dublin, a vibrant tapestry of green begins to unfold. The air, crisp and expectant, fills with the sounds of laughter and music as the city awakens to its grandest celebration. St. Patrick's Day in Dublin is not merely a day but a symphony of culture, history, and festivity, painting the town in countless shades of emerald. Beyond the grand parade, a world of traditional and contemporary Irish culture awaits you, offering a deeper connection to the heart and soul of the Emerald Isle.

St. Patrick's Day in Dublin: Beyond the Parade

Cultural Events

St. Patrick's Day in Dublin is a showcase of Ireland's rich tapestry of arts and culture, extending far beyond the famous parade. Early in the day, the streets resonate with the rhythmic beats of traditional Irish drums and the lilting melodies of flutes during impromptu music sessions that seem to spring up at every corner. Dance troupes perform in open spaces, their feet tapping out complex rhythms, a testament to Ireland's enduring love affair with dance. Literary enthusiasts can revel in poetry slams and readings held in cozy venues like the Winding Stair Bookshop, where local poets and storytellers breathe life into Gaelic legends and contemporary tales. These cultural gatherings provide a rare glimpse into the soul of the city, inviting you to experience the St. Patrick's Day that Dubliners hold dear.

Insider Tips

To truly embrace St. Patrick's Day like a local, venture beyond the main thoroughfares thronged with tourists and into the heart of Dublin's neighborhoods. In places like Stoneybatter, a historic area known for its community spirit, local pubs host gatherings where the Guinness flows freely and the welcome is warm. Here, you can listen to old-timers share tales of St. Patrick's Days past, or perhaps join in a traditional singing session. Avoid the typical tourist traps selling mass-produced memorabilia and seek out local artisans instead, perhaps securing a handcrafted Claddagh ring as a more authentic memento. Remember, the true spirit of St. Patrick's Day in Dublin is found not just in grandiose displays but in the simple joy of shared stories and songs.

Family Activities

St. Patrick's Day is a celebration for all ages, and Dublin offers plenty of family-friendly activities that go beyond watching the parade. Many of Dublin's museums, like the Natural History Museum, host special workshops and interactive tours designed for children, making the rich history of Ireland accessible and engaging for young minds. The Ark, a cultural center for children, often organizes creative sessions where kids can learn about Irish folklore and crafts, or even participate in making their own parade costumes. For a quieter day, consider a family picnic in Phoenix Park, one of Europe's largest walled city parks, where deer roam freely and wide open spaces abound for children to play and explore.

Nightlife and Pub Guide

As evening falls, Dublin transforms into a hub of nightlife and celebration. For those looking to experience authentic Irish pub culture, a visit to the historic Temple Bar area is a must, though it's wise to venture to the less crowded pubs just a few streets away where the atmosphere is more relaxed and the music just as lively. Pubs like The Long Hall and The Cobblestone offer a genuine taste of Irish hospitality, with live music that continues late into the night. Here, you can savor a pint of local craft beer or traditional Irish stout as you tap your feet to the rhythm of folk tunes. If you prefer something more upbeat, many clubs and bars in the Harcourt Street area host St. Patrick's Day parties with DJs and dancing that last until the early hours. Wherever you choose to celebrate, ensure you drink responsibly and consider the local custom of buying 'rounds' of drinks if you're in a group. This enriches your experience and fosters a spirit of camaraderie and celebration at the heart of St. Patrick's Day in Dublin.

Literary Festivals: Ireland's Tribute to the Written Word

Ireland, with its rich literary heritage that spans centuries, is a haven for those who revel in the written word. Across the island, from the rugged landscapes of the West to the historic streets of Dublin, literary festivals bloom throughout the year, each offering a unique celebration of literature and storytelling. These festivals not only honor the giants of Irish literature, such as Yeats, Joyce, and Heaney but also shine a light on contemporary authors and emerging voices, weaving together the past and present of Ireland's literary scene.

The Dublin Writers Festival, held annually in June, is a cornerstone event that attracts writers and readers from around the globe. Here, the city that nurtured the talents of Shaw, Swift, and Wilde becomes a stage for a vibrant exchange of ideas. The festival's program is rich with discussions, readings, and debates, featuring international bestsellers alongside local literary heroes. Special events like the Night of Ideas, where philosophers and poets discuss the role of literature in understanding our times, add a unique flavor to the festival, making it a must-visit for anyone passionate about the power of words.

Moving west, the Listowel Writers' Week in County Kerry offers a more intimate gathering in late May, celebrated for its friendly atmosphere and deep literary connections. This festival, running since 1970, has a strong focus on Irish literary traditions and provides a platform for Irish language writers and poets to showcase their work. Workshops here are particularly notable; they cover everything from fiction and poetry writing to storytelling and are often led by authors whose works are deeply rooted in the Irish landscape and its storytelling traditions. These sessions refine skills and inspire participants by connecting them to the lyrical landscape that has influenced so many Irish writers.

Historically significant venues play a pivotal role in these festivals, adding layers of atmospheric depth to literary celebrations. The James Joyce Centre in Dublin, for instance, serves as a focal point during Bloomsday in June, celebrating Joyce's seminal work, "Ulysses." The center, along with other historic venues like the Dublin Castle and the Smock Alley Theatre, hosts readings and performances that echo the rich literary history of the city. These settings, steeped in history, allow attendees to feel a tangible connection to the literary greats who walked the same streets and penned classics that resonate through generations.

Interactive activities form a core part of these festivals, designed to engage attendees in the creative process. The Cork World Book Fest exemplifies this with its blend of book markets, author signings, and interactive workshops where attendees can learn everything from writing craft to bookbinding. Literary tours are also a highlight, guiding visitors through landscapes that inspired iconic works of Irish literature, such as the rugged beauty of Connemara seen through the eyes of Oscar Wilde, or the haunting settings in Dublin that shaped Bram Stoker's "Dracula." These experiences enrich the festival atmosphere and deepen participants' connections to the literature by experiencing firsthand the settings that inspired them.

As you delve into Ireland's literary festivals, you're not just celebrating its storied literary legacy; you're also encouraged to weave your own narratives, inspired by the island's profound history, vibrant culture, and timeless landscapes. Whether you are a budding writer, a literary scholar, or simply a lover of good stories, these festivals offer a gateway to the heart of Ireland's literary heritage, filled with the voices of the past and the vibrant energy of the present, all connected through the love of words.

The Galway Oyster Festival: A Culinary Celebration

Nestled on the rugged west coast of Ireland, Galway becomes the epicenter of a culinary festivity each September, celebrating one of the sea's most cherished treasures during the Galway Oyster Festival. This event, steeped in tradition and brimming with enthusiasm, has grown from humble beginnings in 1954 to become one of the most significant seafood festivals globally. It was initiated by Brian Collins, the manager of the Great Southern Hotel, to extend the tourist season into autumn. What started as a local gathering has transformed into a grand celebration attracting thousands from across the globe, all drawn by the allure of the native Galway oyster. The festival highlights the culinary delight of oysters and emphasizes the importance of sustainable fishing practices in preserving this tradition for future generations. It's a time when the city's streets buzz with excitement and the community's spirit is showcased through its vibrant festivities and warm hospitality.

The festival's schedule is packed with events that cater to both the curious newcomer and the oyster aficionado. One of the highlights is the World Oyster Opening Championship, a fiercely competitive event that attracts the best shuckers from various corners of the world. Competitors are judged on their speed and finesse in shucking oysters, and the energy and skill displayed are as captivating as the sport itself. Another not-to-be-missed experience is the Oyster Trail, a delightful culinary journey through some of Galway's finest establishments. Participants meander through the city's charming streets, sampling oysters in various preparations, each establishment offering its unique twist on this classic delicacy. From fresh oysters served raw on the half shell to those grilled or baked with indulgent toppings, the trail offers a taste of the local cuisine that is both rich in flavor and history.

For those looking to enhance their festival experience with the art of oyster tasting, there are ample opportunities to learn from the experts. Tasting sessions are often accompanied by recommendations on how to best enjoy these bivalves. A key tip is to appreciate the oyster's natural flavors first without additional condiments. When ready to experiment, a small squeeze of lemon can enhance the oyster's freshness, or a dash of Tabasco can add a bit of zest. Pairing oysters with a perfect beverage is also an art; a crisp, dry white wine, such as a local Galway Riesling, or a stout beer can complement the oyster's briny richness. These sessions refine your palate and deepen your appreciation for oyster cultivation and its culinary heritage.

Given the popularity of the Galway Oyster Festival, securing accommodation well in advance is crucial. The city, with its array of hotels, bed and breakfasts, and boutique lodgings, offers something for every taste and budget, but these can fill up quickly due to the festival's draw. Consider staying in accommodations that offer easy access to festival venues and the city's beautiful waterfront. Booking early not only ensures a wider selection of places to stay but often secures better rates. For those looking for an immersive experience, some local accommodations offer special packages that include festival tickets, meals, and even guided tours of the oyster beds, providing a comprehensive way to enjoy this spectacular event.

As Galway comes alive with the sounds, tastes, and joy of the Oyster Festival, participants are swept up in a celebration that goes beyond mere culinary delight, encapsulating a rich tradition that celebrates community, culture, and the natural bounty of the Irish seas. Whether you're here to compete, to savor, or to simply soak in the festive atmosphere, the Galway Oyster Festival promises an experience that's as enriching as it is delightful, set against the backdrop of one of Ireland's most charming cities.

Traditional Music Festivals: The Heartbeat of Ireland

In Ireland, where music flows as freely as the rivers that cross its verdant landscapes, traditional music festivals stand as pillars of cultural heritage and community celebration. These events, scattered across the calendar and the map, offer vibrant venues where the soulful tunes of the fiddle, the rhythmic beats of the bodhrán, and the haunting melodies of the uilleann pipes come to life. Each festival, unique in its setting and atmosphere, invites you to immerse yourself in the living tradition of Irish music, celebrated amidst the laughter and camaraderie of locals and visitors alike.

One of the most iconic of these gatherings is the Fleadh Cheoil na hÉireann, often simply called The Fleadh, which translates to "The Festival of Music". It is the world's largest annual celebration of Irish music, language, song, and dance. This festival is not just an event; it's a phenomenon that moves to a different host town every year, bringing with it a wave of musicians, dancers, and artists. The streets buzz with music as every pub, square, and alleyway becomes a stage for impromptu jam sessions and organized concerts. The atmosphere here is electric, with performances that range from solo instrumentalists to large folk bands, showcasing the diversity and skill of Irish musicianship.

For a more intimate festival experience, the Willie Clancy Summer School, held annually in Milltown Malbay, County Clare, offers a week-long immersion into traditional Irish music and culture. Named after the famed uilleann piper, this event combines a traditional music school with a festival, creating an environment where learning and celebration go hand in hand. Mornings at Willie Clancy are dedicated to instructional classes taught by master musicians, while evenings see the town alive with concerts, dances, and the ever-popular sessions that spill from the pubs onto the streets.

The festival scene in Ireland also offers special workshops that are treasure troves for anyone keen to delve into the art of traditional Irish instruments. At the aforementioned Willie Clancy Summer School, besides the regular classes, there are specialized workshops focusing on instrument maintenance and history, offering insights that deepen the participants' connection to their instruments. The South Sligo Summer School of traditional music in Tubbercurry is another highlight, where workshops allow you to explore various instruments under the guidance of accomplished musicians. These workshops cater to all skill levels, from beginner to advanced, ensuring that everyone can find a way to grow their musical talent.

Participating in these festivals requires an understanding of session etiquette, an unspoken code that governs the conduct in the spontaneous music gatherings that are the heartbeat of these events. If you find yourself in a session, remember that these are communal experiences. Leading a tune implies you are confident the majority of participants can join in. Always be mindful of the balance; it's considered polite to give everyone a chance to lead a tune. Observing before participating is recommended—it helps in understanding the flow and feel of the session. These gatherings are not just about music, but are a celebration of shared culture and mutual respect.

Family inclusion is a cornerstone of Irish music festivals, making them wonderful occasions for visitors of all ages. The Galway Sessions, held in the bustling city of Galway, prides itself on being family-friendly. Here, afternoon concerts and early evening sessions are tailored to be accessible and enjoyable to families, ensuring that the tradition of Irish music is passed to the next generation in a lively and engaging manner. Children's workshops, storytelling sessions, and family-oriented concerts are common, making these festivals a joyous experience for every family member.

As you weave through the tunes and tales of these festivals, each note played on an Irish fiddle or each rhythm beaten on a bodhrán connects you deeper to the rich tapestry of Ireland's musical heritage. These festivals are not just events; they are vibrant celebrations of life, community, and the enduring spirit of Irish music.

The Wild Atlantic Way: A Journey Through Festivals

Imagine tracing the edges of Ireland's rugged coastlines, where the wild Atlantic crashes against ancient cliffs and whispers through quaint villages. This is the Wild Atlantic Way, a spectacular coastal route that stretches over 2,500 kilometers, making it one of the longest defined coastal routes in the world. As you travel, this path not only offers breathtaking views but also a calendar dotted with vibrant local festivals, each celebrating the unique culture and heritage of the Atlantic coast. From the spirited Donegal festivals in the north to the artistic gatherings in the creative heart of Cork in the south, the route serves as a conduit for a myriad of cultural expressions, manifested through music, dance, art, and culinary delights.

Each festival along the Wild Atlantic Way has its own flavor and charm, turning every stop into a celebration of local culture and community spirit. In the spring, the shores near Sligo come alive with the Surf Music Festival, where surf culture and music create a dynamic beachfront atmosphere. Here, attendees not only catch waves but also rhythms, as bands play against the backdrop of stunning sunsets and roaring seas. Moving towards the mid-summer, the Galway International Arts Festival transforms the Bohemian city into a canvas of artistic exhibitions, street performances, and live concerts. This event not only highlights the rich artistic heritage of Galway but also brings international artists and spectators, creating a melting pot of cultures and ideas along Ireland's Atlantic coast.

Traveling the Wild Atlantic Way during these festival times requires some planning, especially if you wish to immerse yourself fully in the experience. For festival camping, it's essential to book your spot early, as these tend to fill up quickly due to the popularity of the festivals. Opt for campsites that offer amenities such as showers and cooking facilities to enhance your comfort during your stay. If camping is not your style, look for guesthouses or B&Bs in nearby towns. Local accommodations often provide a cozy, authentic experience and the chance to engage with locals who can share insights about the festival and other must-visit spots along the coast.

When it comes to cultural immersion, the Wild Atlantic Way offers endless opportunities to delve into Ireland's traditions and contemporary culture. In Dingle, during the Animation Dingle Festival, participate in workshops that bring together animators from around the globe, offering a behind-the-scenes look at film-making and storytelling. Elsewhere, in towns like Kinsale, famous for its culinary prowess, join seafood cookery classes during the Kinsale Gourmet Festival. These classes allow you to learn directly from local chefs who are masters of transforming fresh, local ingredients into dishes that are as delightful to the palate as the festival is to the spirit. In each of these activities, the emphasis is on participation and learning, allowing you to take more than just memories from each festival—you carry away new skills and more profound understanding.

As you continue your travels along the Wild Atlantic Way, let each festival be a gateway to exploring the deeper cultural currents of the towns and villages dotting the coastline. Whether it's by dancing to traditional Irish music, tasting freshly caught seafood, engaging in workshops, or simply mingling with the locals and fellow travelers, the festivals here offer a way to connect deeply with the life and soul of Ireland's Atlantic coast. Each stop brings its own stories and celebrations, inviting you to not just observe but become part of the ongoing narrative of this wild, wonderful way. As the road winds on and the ocean sings its age-old songs, the festivals of the Wild Atlantic Way beckon you to celebrate, learn, and immerse yourself in the vibrant cultural tapestry of Ireland.

Christmas in Ireland: A Magical Season

In the heart of winter, Ireland transforms into a festive wonderland, where the crisp air is infused with the scent of peat fires and spiced mulled wine. Cities like Dublin, Belfast, and Galway dress in their holiday best, with Christmas markets that beckon with twinkling lights and cheerful music. The ambiance of these markets is a blend of old-world charm and festive cheer. Dublin's Christmas Market on Grafton Street offers an enchanting experience where wooden chalets brim with artisan crafts and holiday treats. Here, you can find hand-knitted woolens perfect for the chilly Irish winter or choose from an array of handmade jewelry and crafts for unique Christmas gifts. In Belfast, the market at City Hall delights visitors with an array of international cuisines, from Belgian chocolates to German bratwurst, reflecting the city's cosmopolitan spirit. The Galway Christmas Market, set in Eyre Square, is a family favorite, featuring a traditional carousel, live music performances, and an appearance from Santa Claus himself, creating a joyful atmosphere that captures the magic of the season.

The celebration of Christmas in Ireland is steeped in unique traditions that mirror the country's rich cultural tapestry. One of the most intriguing is Wren Day, traditionally observed on December 26th, St. Stephen's Day. This peculiar tradition involves 'hunting' a fake wren, and parading it around the village. Participants, called 'wrenboys', dress in straw masks and colorful motley clothes, singing and dancing from house to house to raise funds for community projects. Another deeply cherished tradition is the midnight Mass on Christmas Eve, a spiritual gathering where families unite to celebrate the birth of Christ. It's a poignant moment, often illuminated by candlelight, where the harmonies of traditional carols like "Silent Night" resonate in the arches of churches filled with the community spirit.

The festive season is also a time to indulge in the culinary delights that are quintessentially Irish. Mince pies, with their rich filling of fruits, nuts, and spices encased in a buttery pastry, are a staple on any Irish Christmas table. These treats are best enjoyed with a dollop of brandy butter or a cup of hot tea. Another traditional favorite is spiced beef, an aromatic and savory dish that features heavily in Christmas feasts, particularly in Cork. This seasoned and cured beef is cooked slowly to perfection, served cold in thin slices, and is often accompanied by chutney or mustard. For those eager to try these festive foods, local bakeries and markets are the best places to find them, offering freshly made pies and locally cured meat that embody the flavors of the season.

One of the most mystical experiences of the Irish Christmas season is the Winter Solstice at Newgrange, a Neolithic passage tomb located in County Meath. This ancient site dates back over 5,000 years, older than Stonehenge and the Great Pyramids of Giza. Each year, during the winter solstice, something magical occurs – the rising sun aligns perfectly with the passage tomb, illuminating its inner chamber with a golden glow. This event is a profound connection to Ireland's ancient past, and witnessing it is a once-in-a-lifetime experience that draws visitors from around the world. Entry to the chamber during the solstice is determined by a lottery system, which you can enter via the Brú na Bóinne Visitor Centre. Those who win the chance to experience this ancient wonder will find themselves part of a timeless ritual that continues to captivate and mystify.

As this chapter draws to a close, reflecting on the vibrant celebrations and unique traditions of an Irish Christmas offers a deeper appreciation for the rich cultural fabric of this nation. From the bustling Christmas markets and the family gatherings at midnight Mass to the ancient rituals at Newgrange, Ireland during the festive season is a tapestry of old and new, sacred and celebratory. Each tradition and celebration is a thread in the larger story of Ireland, inviting you to experience the warmth and joy of an Irish Christmas. As we turn the page to the next chapter, we carry forward the spirit of celebration and community that embodies the Irish approach to life and festivity.

CONCLUSION

As we draw the curtains on this written journey through the verdant fields and vibrant streets of Ireland, I hope you have felt the misty breezes of the Atlantic and heard the lilting tunes of a fiddle carried through the cobblestone alleys. We've traversed from the majestic Cliffs of Moher to the serene pathways of Connemara, delving into the hidden gems and cultural bastions that make Ireland an endlessly fascinating country. Each chapter aimed to unveil not just the scenic beauty but the soul of Ireland —its people, traditions, and stories.

Throughout this book, we've explored the richness of Ireland's landscapes, the significant historical and cultural landmarks that narrate centuries-old tales, and the modern culinary revolution that invites your palate to a feast of flavors. We discussed practical advice for navigating the varied terrain of this beautiful island, from bustling city streets to tranquil coastal paths. More importantly, we connected with the spirit of the Irish people, whose hospitality and warmth make every visit memorable.

Travel, as we've seen, is more than just an escape from the everyday; it's a gateway to personal transformation and cultural enlightenment. Ireland, with its blend of ancient traditions and contemporary dynamism, offers a unique canvas for these experiences. Whether you're an adventurer eager to explore the untamed Wild Atlantic Way, a history enthusiast unraveling the layers of Ireland's past, a foodie indulging in epicurean delights, or a family looking for a magical holiday, Ireland welcomes all with open arms and a warm heart.

In your travels, I urge you to tread lightly and lovingly. Embrace responsible tourism by respecting natural landscapes, supporting local artisans and businesses, and engaging with the community in a way that enriches both your experience and the locales you visit. Let's ensure that the emerald sheen of this island remains vibrant for generations to come, preserving its beauty and spirit.

Now, I invite you not just to dream of Ireland, but to step into its reality. Use this book as your companion and guide. Go off the beaten path, engage deeply with the culture, and let Ireland transform you, just as it has countless wanderers before. Your adventure awaits, filled with tales yet to be told and memories waiting to be made.

Thank you for sharing this journey with me. I hope you've been inspired, informed, and intrigued. As we part ways in this concluding chapter, I leave you with a personal reflection: Ireland, to me, is more than just a destination; it's a feeling—a pulse of life, history, and nature dancing together. It's a land where each stone, stream, and song has a story waiting to be discovered. May this book serve as your gateway to those stories, guiding you to find the magic that Ireland holds. Safe travels, and may the road rise up to meet you.

REFERENCES

7 Hidden Gems in Connemara https://www.sheepandwoolcentre.com/blogs/news/7-hidden-gems-in-connemara

Your Guide To Surfing In Sligo With Discover Ireland https://www.discoverireland.ie/sligo/surfing-sligo

Burren LIFE: Farming for Conservation https://www.catchments.ie/burren-life-farming-conservation/

Titanic Experience Cobh: Visit Titanic's last port of call https://www.titanicexperiencecobh.ie

Russell Festival Doolin – Traditional Irish Music Festival in ... https://russellfestivalweekend.ie/

Gaelic Athletic Association https://en.wikipedia.org/wiki/Gaelic_Athletic_Association

How To Celebrate Bloomsday 2023 in Dublin https://www.visitdublin.com/guides/bloomsday-guide

10 great whiskey distillery tours around Ireland https://www.ireland.com/en-us/magazine/food-and-drink/10-great-whiskey-distillery-tours/

The Complete Wicklow Way Trail Blog https://blog.hiiker.app/2020/02/14/the-complete-wicklow-way-trail-blog/

Starlight kayaking on Ireland's glow-in-the-dark lake https://www.image.ie/living/starlight-kayaking-corks-glow-dark-lake-130902

Cliffs of Moher: 4 Unique Ways to See 'em in 2024 https://www.theirishroadtrip.com/cliffs-of-moher-ireland/

Tips for Biking the Great Western Greenway in Ireland https://www.polkadotchair.com/biking-the-great-western-greenway-in-ireland/

What to Wear in Ireland: Month-by-Month Ireland Packing ... https://irelandfamilyvacations.com/ireland-vacation-clothing-tips/ireland-travel-tips/

Hiking in Ireland? We Detail What to Wear https://www.wildernessireland.com/blog/what-to-wear-hiking-in-ireland

THE 10 BEST Indoor Things to Do in Ireland (Updated 2024) https://www.tripadvisor.com/Attractions-g186591-Activities-zft11295-Ireland.html

The Ultimate Packing List for Ireland (+ What to Wear!) https://www.ourescapeclause.com/packing-list-for-ireland/

Everything You Need to Know About Car Rental in Ireland ... https://irelandfamilyvacations.com/car-rental-ireland/ireland-travel-tips/

Public transport in Ireland https://en.wikipedia.org/wiki/Public_transport_in_Ireland

On your bike – 8 of Ireland's best cycling routes https://www.discoverireland.ie/guides/ireland-best-cycling-routes

Our Favourite Islands off the Coast of Ireland https://vagabondtoursofireland.com/blog/best-islands-visit-coast-ireland

The Best Castle Hotels in Ireland https://www.cntraveler.com/gallery/the-best-castle-hotels-in-ireland

Snuggle up in Irish cottages https://www.vrbo.com/vacation-ideas/vacation-rentals/unique/cottages-and-farms/irish-cottage

24 BEST Hostels in Ireland (2024 Insider Guide) https://www.thebrokebackpacker.com/best-hostels-in-ireland/

Sustainable stays https://www.ireland.com/plan-your-trip/accommodation/sustainable-stays-in-ireland/

Cheesemakers - Irish Cheese https://irish-cheese.com/cheesemakers-list/

About Irish Breweries and Distilleries https://www.myirelandtour.com/travelguide/culture/breweries-and-distilleries.php

The Best Seafood Restaurants in the Republic of Ireland https://guide.michelin.com/us/en/best-of/best-of-fish-and-seafood-restaurants-in-the-republic-of-ireland

Ballymaloe Cookery School https://www.ballymaloecookeryschool.ie/

Events & Parade | St. Patrick's Festival | 15 – 18 March 2024 https://stpatricksfestival.ie/events

Writing Festivals in Ireland https://www.writing.ie/resources/writing-festivals-in-ireland/

About GIOF | Galway International Oyster Festival https://www.galwayoysterfestival.com/about-giof/

10 BEST traditional Irish music festivals in Ireland (2024) https://www.irelandbeforeyoudie.com/top-10-best-traditional-irish-music-festivals-in-ireland-ranked/

Made in the USA
Las Vegas, NV
24 February 2025

18660048R00085